Klaus-Thorsten Tegge

Diving around

GOZO

Impressum

Klaus-Thorsten Tegge - **Diving around Gozo**

Many Thanks -
to everyone who helped me to complete this book.

The author was born 1961 in Hamburg, Germany, and has been diving since 1977. Klaus is a CMAS/VDST-instructor** in the "Deutscher Unterwasser Club Hamburg /VDST". He is able to combine his profession as an Environmental technology engineer at the department of the environment in Hamburg with his favourite element "water". Spending a lot of his spare time he tries to make the public more aware of environmental problems. In 1984 Klaus discovered Gozo during his travels and has spent numerous vacations and educational trips on this beautiful Maltese Island, ever since.

Contact:
info@dive-gozo.com
www.dive-gozo.com

This book was translated from the 3rd German edition "Tauchen auf Gozo" with the assistance of Lars Frehse, Christian Trowitzsch, Kevin White and other friends.

Fabrication and publisher: Books on Demand GmbH Norderstedt, Germany
Printed in Germany ISBN 978-3831147533

Finally I'm back again! A blast of heat welcomes me as I leave the aircraft at Luqa, Malta's international airport. I know that in only a few hours I can start the first dive in the crystal water of the Maltese Archipelago. As usual, there is a taxi driver waiting to pick me up - is it the same guy as last time? He will drive me to Cirkewwa harbour where I will board a ferry to Gozo a small neighbouring island of Malta. When discussing my holiday plans nobody seems to have heard of this idyllic island. However, Gozo is meanwhile becoming well known as an insider tip among divers.

Although not as colourful as the Red Sea, and perhaps not as rich in species as other parts of the Mediterranean, Gozo's underwater landscape is spectacular and the waters surrounding the island are of the most beautiful blue that I have ever seen. Gozo has a number of scenic dive sites that lie closely together, far away from the bustling tourism, which is ever present on the main island. Hopefully it will remain this way.

I'm happy to leave the noisy main island and to finally board the ferry for the half-hour crossing to Mgarr, Gozo's main harbour. The ferry has completed this journey thousands of times over the years and despite her appearance I'm sure she will make it again! It isn't just the diving that fascinates me but also the solitude of Gozo's open landscape.

There are ten dive shops operating on the island that adequately cater for all diving requirements, with various packages and offers.

Gozo is a popular and cheap holiday destination, in particular for experienced divers that wish to dive independently. Using rental cars and dive tanks, one can dive almost everywhere. Early morning or midnight dives are no problem for those divers who know the location. The aim of this guide is to give the reader the information necessary for these dives. I hope that the following explanations will help you to discover Gozo so that on your next visit you, too, will think: "Finally I'm back again"!

Enjoy your stay on Gozo

Klaus-Thorsten Tegge

Preface 2nd. edition:
Meanwhile I have been staying regularly on Gozo for 15 years and have - so my hopes - helped a lot of divers with the information of my guidebook. This long period didn't pass by Gozo without changes, positive and also negative. The connection to the main island became much faster and comfortable, the roads are in better conditions and the touristic supply is more completed. The full membership to the EU brought the Euro and many other adaptations to European standards.

We can see some of the changes as a disadvantage. Gozo isn't that slumbering island that it was 20 years ago. But I think, and hope that the most Gozo fans will agree, that the kindnesses of the island still exist. Also the deserted recreation areas (except in the high season) didn't disappear. Certainly this is correct for diving! In the same meaning, this new edition has the same idea as it predecessor but has a lot of small updates and - for the first time - coloured pictures.

Contents

Diving on Gozo is both beautiful and fascinating. But what exactly awaits the diver? This guide starts with general information about diving conditions. Next follows - as the heart of this book - a detailed description of each diving site. Safety precautions are also included plus some information and hints for "après diving", i.e. suggestions regarding what to do and where to go after the dive. A detailed location map is included with the description for each dive.

This is followed by a brief overview of Gozo's population, history, culture and points of interest that should give you an impression of the island. Besides diving it should also encourage visitors to discover the beauty of Gozo. Tips concerning travel, weather, addresses, internet links and other useful information are detailed in the next section.

The marine fauna and flora of the Maltese islands have been intentionally neglected. It is almost biologically identical to other areas of the Mediterranean and already well documented in numerous other books. Some recommendable biology guides are mentioned in the bibliography at the end of the book. There are also some more reading tips concerning diving and travel.

In case of an emergency immediate help is vital. For this purpose emergency procedures are printed on the last page of this guide. N.B. make a copy and take it with you whenever you dive.

You can find more information and the possibility to order the DVD to this book with many scenes of the dive sites of Gozo and much more on my website www.dive-gozo.com.

Diving on Gozo

General Information

Gozo is easy to grasp, a "small" yellow limestone rock reaching up to 176 m out of the sea. The rugged coastlines with many sheer cliffs that drop vertically from 160 m to almost 40 m below sea level are the main characteristics of this 15 km by 7 km island. In between, there are areas where the land slopes gently down to the sea. The 7 miniature "table mountains" dominate on the landscape and lend Gozo the nickname "the island of the seven hills".

In the centre of the island is Victoria (in Maltese: Rabat) the island's capital with a large fortress (Citadel) that dominates the town. A network of narrow bumpy roads head out in all directions to the surrounding villages that are either exposed on the hills or hidden in the small bays along the 43 km coastline. Further characteristic landmarks are the domes of the numerous churches.

In contrast to other Mediterranean islands it is common on Gozo to dive from the shore. There are many sites along the coastline that can be easily reached by car. Diving at these sites can be done either independently or with the assistance of one of the local diving schools.

Diving regulations

Local regulations stipulate that divers without 2-star certification, i.e. CMAS** or PADI AOWD, may only dive when accompanied by an instructor with a local license. In case of an elementary qualification all shore and boat dives must be made with licensed guides. During the high season diving takes place mainly in large groups. This may not suit everyone, but during the low season, when things are quieter, visitors may often have their own personal guide. Particularly during the low season, qualified **divers wishing to join a diving school can normally dive independently away from the "rowdy" group. Beginners must first graduate from an elementary course. All schools offer a range of courses from elementary up to advanced; some are also certified to train instructor levels. N.B. All divers will need to present a valid medical certificate,

Diving independently/ in groups

Divers who possess at least a 2-star-qualification are permitted to dive independently without a local guide. They only need to sign on to a registered diving school. There they have to present beside a valid medical certificate the logbook and evidence of at least a 2-star-diver certification.

Tanks, weights and any other necessary utensils may be hired from the diving schools. A rental car will also be required to reach the diving sites. Diving is permitted almost anywhere at any time. There are, however, two exceptions: firstly Ramla Bay and on the south side of the entrance to Xlendi Bay, where archaeological discoveries are being investigated and therefore diving is not allowed. Furthermore the diving site at Ta'Cenc is situated on private land where local regulations must be observed [-> diving site Ta'Cenc]. And lastly although greater depths are possible, dives should not exceed 40 m!

Advice: though it is allowed to dive unaccompanied as pronounced before, I recommend divers who stay the first time on Gozo to join the rides with a dive centre

Diving on Gozo

and dive accompanied, at least for some dives to get to know the local diving conditions. Doing the first dives with an experienced guide is safer and much more relaxed. And you can concentrate your senses on the beautiful underwater world of Gozo.

Diving conditions

Under normal conditions the visibility is usually at least 25 meters, but quite often 40 meters and more! Visibility, however, may be affected by rainfall washing the soft limestone into the sea. The water will then be very milky around the inlets and visibility minimal. Storms with strong waves can stir up the seabed and also reduce visibility. Fortunately bad weather is rare in the main season from April to November [-> climate & weather]. Where the shore drops off (e.g. Reqqa Point) and no streams flow into the sea, the visibility is hardly affected by weather.

Apart from the excellent visibility, the numerous drop-offs are characteristic for the island. At these marvellous diving sites it is possible to attain great depths very quickly. Attention! Plan the dive carefully. Observe the agreed maximum depth! Dives to extreme depths can easily lead to problems: e.g. nitrogen narcosis, lack of air or long decompressions. Please consider that 50% of all decompression accidents are caused by lack of air. However, the sensible diver who critically judges his own capabilities and those of his partner (!) can experience fantastic dives on Gozo's drop-offs.

Many canyons and giant rocks beneath the surface are really impressive. In addition there are also numerous caves. These often have a wide entrance that open up into giant caverns. Some of these caves are relatively simple to dive so that even beginners can gain their first experiences there. In those caves there is sufficient light available so that the exit is always visible and divers can navigate without a lamp. Nevertheless, it is still absolutely essential to have a lamp available. Obviously, due to the additional dangers involved, careful planning is necessary.

Diver at Calypso Tunnel

Divers should not proceed further into any of the tunnel systems when they become narrow or poorly lit. Only divers with additional pot-holing/ diving experience are permitted to continue the dive. Fortunately many spectacular caves and tunnels are relatively simple to dive and therefore recommendable.

Gozo offers a multitude of possibilities like cave and night diving, underwater photography or marine biology. However, it does not offer wrecks or drift diving. For extensive wreck diving Malta presents a number of interesting alternatives. Currents around

Gozo are seldom and when they occur they are usually weak e.g. at exposed places like North Comino Channel or on the coastline off Reqqa Point [-> description of the dive sites].

There were no wrecks on the Gozo coastline until in 1999 when the scrapped car ferry "Xlendi" was intentionally sunk off the south coast near Mellieha Point. Unfortunately the sinking operation failed and the "Xlendi" sank headfirst, settling wide of the designated position in approximately 40 m. After 10 years in this position the wreck became more and more unstable and it is now very dangerous to dive inside. So diving is only allowed outside of this vessel. But nearby two additional ships were sunk in 2006 [-> Diving place 14. Xatt l-Ahmar], offering wreck enthusiast reasonable objects. For extensive wreck diving Malta presents a number of interesting alternatives.

Another aspect to be considered when selecting a dive site is the access to the water, i.e. how to get in and how to get out. There are various entrances available, e.g. flat gravel beaches, slippery jetties, long staircases or risky climbs combined with

daredevil jumps. With the necessary caution most of these places are accessible for everybody. This poses the next question: "are the current conditions suitable for a save dive?". This should obviously be clarified before suiting up.

Winds cause a turbulent sea on the north coast

Sudden wind changes can increase wave movement so that entrance and exit points at some dive sites can quickly become difficult. N.B. the diver can probably get into the water easily enough but he should not forget that he also has to be able to exit at the same point. Often there may be no alternative exits available! This is particularly important as the sea may get rougher during the dive, which could easily result in a dangerous situation!

Attention! It is helpful to check both the wind and the latest weather report (ask your dive centre) before planning the dives. A lot of diving places are very dependent on wind conditions. Even soft breezes can create strong wave movement, which makes the entrance into the water more difficult or even impossible. N.B. unprotected entrances on windward sites are affected strongest.

The marine world / Biology

Following stormy weather a strong swell can affect the access for some days. Fortunately the island is rather small and an alternative dive site is always available. In case of doubt, it is always better to switch rather to take an unnecessary risk! Imagine a wave lifting a diver 2 m into a jagged crack and then suddenly subsiding causing the diver to crash on to the rocks below. Injuries and damaged equipment are inevitable. But in general diving on Gozo is not difficult assuming one observes the usual precaution because bad weather, particularly during the main season, is rare.

The marine world

As already mentioned Gozo's underwater world is extremely versatile. There are many very impressive rock faces that drop-off to depths of 40 m and more. These walls can be found at both the exit of the Inland Sea and on the whole of the north-west coastline. Many drop-offs start beneath the surface e.g. between Xwieni Bay and Reqqa Point, where a plateau extends throughout the shallow area and later drops off sharply to 35 m. At the foot of the drop-off the sandy seabed slopes down further into the depths. Sometimes one may find giant boulders below these walls that have parted from the mainland. Not all are derived from prehistoric times. As an example: In comparison with older pictures of the Azure Window one finds a large gap in the arc. The missing rock can be found on the seabed directly beneath the window.

Deep dives are not necessary to find beautiful caves. Some can be found in shallow waters. These were washed out of the soft Gozo limestone in prehistoric times. Apart from huge "concert hall" sized caves there are also numerous smaller caves, many of which extend far into the stone. When a cave is running more or less upright it is referred to as a chimney. A number of beautiful examples exist left of the Blue Hole and also at Reqqa Point. Equally interesting are the horizontal tunnels e.g. one is connected to the "Chimney" at the Blue Hole. A slightly larger example can be found at Xlendi bay. The canyon-like tunnel between the Inland Sea and the open water is the largest on Gozo. Further canyons can be found at Ghasri Valley and Mgarr Ix-Xini where the shore drops steeply into a spectacular landscape.

The giant arc of the Azure Window is unique where one can dive around the pillar. Although smaller, the double arch at Xwieni Bay is equally beautiful. These two openings in a narrow wall are located at about 30 m north-west of Xwieni Bay. Several rocks jut up out of the sea - the largest of these are Fungus Rock and Fessej Rock - to complete an assortment of natural monuments. The area around the Blue Hole must be mentioned here as it offers an extravagant combination of vertical walls, chimneys, arches and caves.

Those who like the shallow sandy areas and meadows of sea-grass will find ample opportunities all around the island. Under the motto "The underwater desert is alive" one can expect to discover several species that would not be found in rocky places. This can more than compensate for the sometimes monotonous surroundings.

Biology of the Maltese sea

Gozo's marine flora and fauna is typical for the Mediterranean. The Gozo coastline offers a wide variety of habitats so that every dive becomes a voyage of discove-

ry. Numerous colourful small fish populate the drop-offs. At greater depths one may occasionally find large grouper. Looking up to the surface, one can sometimes see shoals of barracuda or garfish hunting above you. If you search carefully between the rocks, you may also find moray eels. Various species of stingray are indigenous to Gozo. From time to time one should also have a look down into the Big Blue and with luck one may discover sharks or tuna patrolling the deeper water. Shoals of jack or sardine can be observed more frequently. Divers who wish to observe the whole variety of bryozoans must get closer to the grown rocky walls.

Numerous forms of algae, sponges, worms and echinoderms are living there. In shadowed areas the diver often finds wide colonies of yellow cub corals and red corals. In the more protected areas, e.g. in caves, one may find a selection of tube-worms and anemones. You will almost certainly find a variety of hermit crabs, snails and some beautiful nudibranchs together with the omnipresent rag worms moving between the rocks where the green bonellia are searching for food with their long snouts.

An encounter with the common cuttlefish is normal on almost every dive. The common octopus is by comparison harder to find in its rocky hiding-place at daylight, but at night they are more frequently seen as they come out to hunt. In the dark the diver is more likely to discover the giant ton, as they glide over the sandy bottom with surprising speed. This extraordinary diverse region offers a multitude of species: e.g. plaice, stingray, stargazer, gurnard, shell, starfish, crabs and worms. The sandy seabed is often covered with sea-grass. It is the ideal habitat for pipefish and sea hor-

ses. It is rewarding to take along a detailed biology guide in order to identify the species discovered after the dive [-> Bibliography].

Boat dives/ diving on Malta and Comino

Although there are plenty of sites with shore accessibility, there are far more that cannot be reached from land. Great areas along the coastline are only accessible by boat, especially the steep coastline in the north and south-west where the diver finds impressive drop-offs and caves.

Divers wishing to dive these sites are recommended to join one of the regular boat dives offered by local dive shops. It is also possible to rent a boat, thus organising trips on your own. Although these trips are a little more expensive, it is advisable for all divers who wish to avoid climbing or long distance snorkelling. As an alternative to normal shore dives a boat trip is recommended for everyone. However, one should not expect to find a totally different underwater landscape. In addition to Gozo there are other beautiful places for diving on Malta and Comino. Apart from wreck dives around Malta there are no further sensational attractions. On Malta there is always more bustle, also at diving places. There are more than 20 diving facilities and subsequently a lot of divers, too. The number of diving places on Malta is equal to Gozo. Special attention is drawn to Migra Ferha - a famous drop-off down at Dingli Cliffs as well as to the "Blenheim Bomber" on the east coast of Malta. As a witness of the combat of Valetta some wrecks (HMS Maori and Carolina) lie on the seabed in Valletta Harbour. These are attractive dive sites but generally there is poor visibility. A further favourite is the wreck of the "Um El Faroud" on the south coast of Malta. Some more recent wrecks compliment the offer. Very popular is the wreck Rozi near the harbour of Cirkewwa. Since the summer of 2007 it is neighboured by the P29, the old patrol boat "Boltenhagen" from Germany.

Recommendable is a day trip to Comino that is surrounded by crystal clear water. This is the smallest of the three populated islands of the archipelago that is located between Malta and Gozo. The favourite destinations for boat dives are the Santa Marija Cave and the Lantern Reef. Between dives the Blue Lagoon offers everybody the chance to swim or picnic. There are doubts whether of the same name movie was really filmed there because of the absence of palm trees.

The bays of Comino

Diving centres

Nowadays there are about 12 diving centres offering their services on Gozo. Apart from supplying air, tank hire and other diving equipment, they also organise daily tours to dive sites by car or boat. In addition, they also offer diving education and special courses usually along PADI guidelines, but also there are also opportunities to facilitate other diving organisations, e.g. CMAS or BSAC.

Apart from air supply, many of the centres offer Nitrox and sometimes also Oxygen or Trimix as technical diving is becoming more popular. The range of offers is often extended with specials courses in Nitrox- or technical diving. Most of the diving facilities also offer bed and breakfast, airport

transfers and car rentals as packages. Therefore, it is convenient to use one partner to book the entire vacation, possibly making it cheaper, too.

Atlantis Diving
Qolla Street, Marsalforn, MFN 1405, Gozo
Tel: (00356) 21 55 4685,
Fax: 21 555661, Mobile: 7971 0390,
Email: info@atlantisgozo.com
www.atlantisgozo.com

This facility is managed by Stephania and Brian Azzorpardi and my personal recommendation. Complete supply for all kind of divers. Shop, airport transportation, agency for all categories of acommodations (own cheap apartments). Diving guidelines: PADI (5star IDC), BSAC, CMAS in English, German, French, Dutch and Italian. Nitrox and trimix supply.

Diving centres

Blue Waters Dive Cove

Kuncizzjoni Street, Qala, Gozo, GSM 103, Malta. Tel: (00356) 21 565626, Mobile: 99 224114. Email: info@divebluewaters.com
www.bluewaters.com

New diving centre in Quala near Mgarr, away from touristic paths. Diving courses, excursions, tourist service. Diving guidelines: Padi in English, German and Italian.

Calypso Diving Centre

Marsalforn Bay Seafront, Gozo, Malta
Tel: (00356) 21 561757, Fax: 21 562020
Email: info@calypsodivers.com
www.calypsodivers.com

The diving school belongs to the Calypso Hotel which is located at the harbour of Marsalforn. Shop, own dive boat, packages. Diving guidelines: PADI, BSAC in English, Italian and German.

Extra Divers

St. Anthony Street, Ghanjsielem, Gozo, Malta. Tel: (00356) 2155 6183, Fax: 2155 9744. Email: extradivers@grandhotelmalta.com
www.extradiversgozo.com

A small dive school guided by a German Instructor. The small but tidy centre is connected to the Grand Hotel in Ghanjsielem above the harbour of Mgarr.

Frankie's Gozo Diving Centre

Mgarr Road, Xewkija, Gozo, Malta
Tel: (00356) 21 551315, Fax: 21 560356
Mobile: 99 497757, Email:
info@gozodiving.com
www.gozodiving.com

The dive centre is located at the main road from Mgarr to Victoria and has new German speaking owners since 2008. Janet and Oliver offer a wide variety of services, including cruises around the Maltese archipelago. Diving guidelines: PADI in English, Italian, French, Dutch and German.

Gozo Aqua Sports

Green Valley, Rabat Road, Marsalforn, MFN 9014. Tel: (00356) 21 563037, Fax: 21 559938. Email: dive@gozoaquasports.com
www.gozoaquasports.com

PADI 5-Star centre with many different services also offering a children's nursery facility. Diving guidelines: PADI and BSAC in English, Dutch and German.

Moby Dives

Tradewinds Bldg, Triq il-Gostra, Xlendi VCT 115. Tel: (00356) 21 564429, Fax: 21 554606. Mobile: 99 499595,
Email: info@mobydivesgozo.com
www.mobydive.com

Located directly at the Xlendi Bay this centre offers own accommodation and restaurant besides the diving school. Indoor Pool, Shop, handicapped diving. Diving guidelines: PADI, SAA, SSI, IDD, IAHD (Int. Ass. Of Handicapped Divers) in English, Dutch, Norwegian and German.

Nautic Team Gozo

Volcano Street, Marsalforn, Gozo, Malta
Tel&Fax: (00356) 21 558 507
Email: nauticteam@fastnet.net.mt
www.nauticteam.com

A German run diving facility in the centre of Marsalforn. Wide range of courses, Nitrox fillings, children diving, handicapped diving. Diving guidelines: CMAS, Barakuda, PADI, SSI in German, English, Spanish and French.

Scuba Kings

46A Triq Marina, Marsalforn Seafront, Marsalforn
Mobile: (00356) 99 230788
Email: gozodiveschool@hotmail.com
www.divemalta-gozo.com

Small dive centre at the waterfront of Marsalforn. Philosophy: special arrangements for small groups, Diving guidelines: PADI, BSAC.

St. Andrew's Divers Cove
St. Simon Street, Xlendi Bay, Gozo XLN 1302
Tel: (00356) 21 551301, Fax: 21 561548
Email: standrew@gozodive.com
www.gozodive.com

This facility with good sorted shop is located directly at the Xlendi Bay and offers e.g. NITROX, speciality courses and complete packages. Diving guidelines: PADI, CMAS in English, Italian, French, Flemish and German.

Utina Diving College
Rabat Road, Xlendi XLN 1101, Gozo, Malta.
Tel&Fax: (00356) 21 550514, Mobile: 79 550514
Email: utina@gozomail.com
www.utina-diving.com

Slogan: Size is everything and Utina is very small. Diving guidelines: PADI, ITDA (technical diving) in English.

Prices at diving schools are all in the same range, but there are differences between the various packages offered. Most of the diving centres offer special courses (e.g. cave diving or marine biology) and some centres also cater for all-day-trips and other special arrangements. Do not hesitate to mention any special requirements.

Independent self-sufficient divers are not appreciated everywhere. Some dive centres are reluctant to offer information or tank filling facilities to persons not using their centre. The best way is to ask other divers and learn from their experience.

For dive holidays my personal recommendation is to stay in either Marsalforn or Xlendi. Both places offer diving centres, shopping areas and restaurants as well as a friendly atmosphere. The beautiful promenades are ideal for a romantic sunset on the beach: a guarantee for the real holiday feeling.

Snorkelling

Many of the diving sites can be equally well discovered without tanks. Using simple snorkel gear (ABC) one can easily observe the marine world in the shallow coastal areas. Accompanying non-divers won't have to wait on the beach as even with limited swimming capabilities they can observe their diving friends or discover the marine world below.

Snorkellers have fun on Gozo, too

Though the use of ABC-equipment is relatively simple, it is recommended to first practice at home in your local swimming pool, before progressing to the sea. A degree of fitness is also essential. One shouldn't snorkel alone! Snorkelling with a partner is safer and also more fun. When diving sites are suitable for snorkelling there are specific hints in the site-description.

N.B. do not forget a waterproof sun tan lotion. However, the best way to avoid sunburn is to wear a T-shirt!

Further important information

Do not underestimate the strength of the sun. It is far too easy to get sunburned and/or dehydrated. Particularly during high-summer Gozo may become very hot.

A few simple rules:

1. Avoid dehydration. Drink sufficient quantities of mineral water or juice!

2. Take drinks with you. Drink before you get thirsty!

N.B. dehydration not only disturbs the circulation but can also increase the liability to caisson illness (decompression sickness).

3. Avoid unnecessary exposure to the sun!

4. Avoid stress situations!

5. Avoid strenuous marches to the dive entry points in neoprene!

6. Take care of your partner as much as yourself!

The heat may tempt the diver to swap a thick suit for a T-shirt. Don't underestimate the danger of hypothermia, particularly in early summer when the temperature of the sea is still below 20°C! It is a well-known fact that the human body loses more warmth in water than in the air. A typical situation: first sweating and then later shivering during the dive. If you catch cold you might not be able to dive for the next couple of days. A warm suit and gloves are recommended until the end of May, especially for frequent dives.

One further important tip: For those who prefer to dive barefoot wearing pool fins beware! Entry and exit points often involve climbing over jagged rocks. To avoid injuries always wear firm shoes (booties) to entry points. The more sensible diver wears boots with firm soles that can be worn with your fins. Gloves and knee protection are recommended to protect your hands and diving suit during any climbing activities. This protection should not mislead one to neglect the well-known underwater rules: "don't touch, don't damage!".

Fishing and boating are the favourite activities of the Gozitians. Boat propellers and fishing lines present constant dangers for divers. In open water there is the danger of fishing nets. Dive carefully! Paying attention to your surroundings, constantly checking for fishing lines etc. will help to minimise the risk of critical situations. A Maltese regulation stipulates that divers should carry a marker buoy. This is however frequently ignored. At places with frequent boat traffic it is recommended to use a signal buoy.

A final hint: it is useful to take a rope to places where the diver is planning to jump into the water because he can lower down sensitive equipment such as lamps, cameras etc. . Of course a strong rope can also be very helpful when leaving the water, especially in high waves, e.g. at Reqqa Point or Ta'Cenc after the ladder has been removed (late afternoon). The rope must be secured in a way that you can pull yourself out. It also can be of some use for rescue actions. Otherwise this can be very difficult when steep exits are involved.

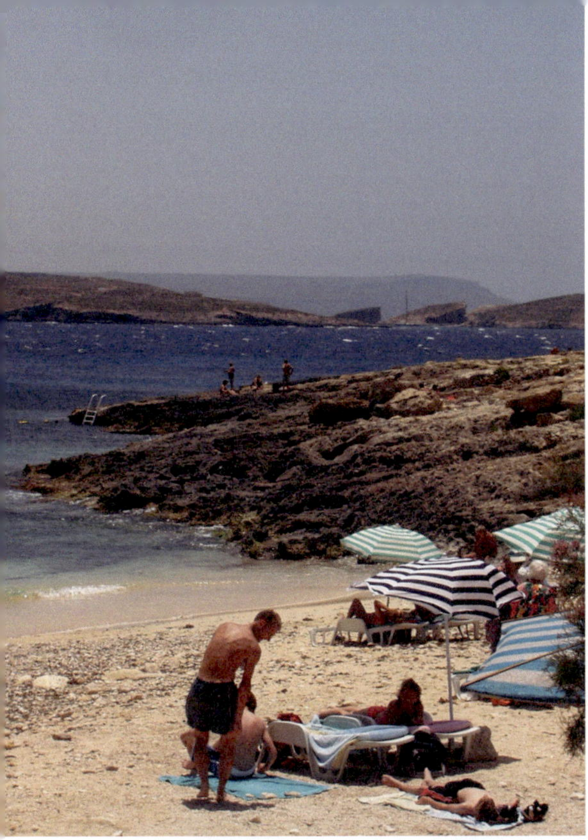
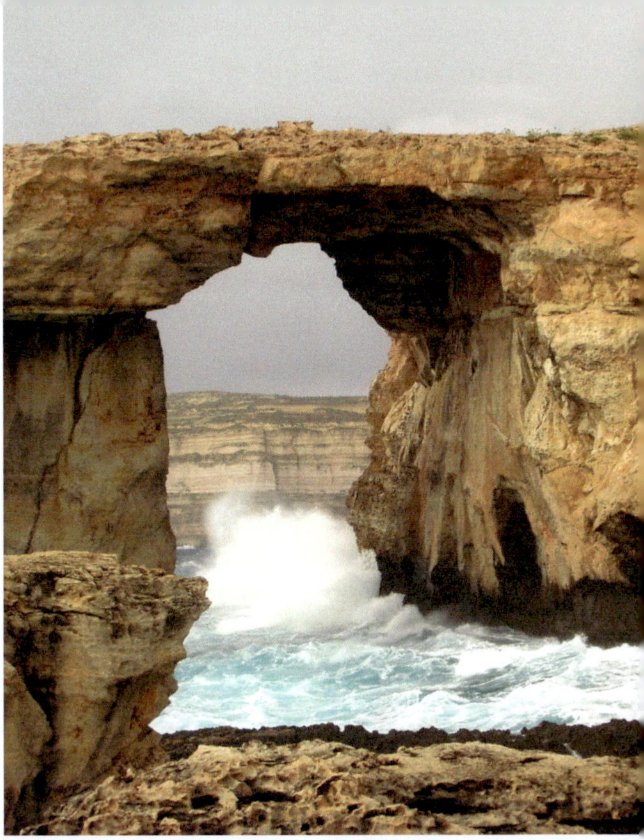
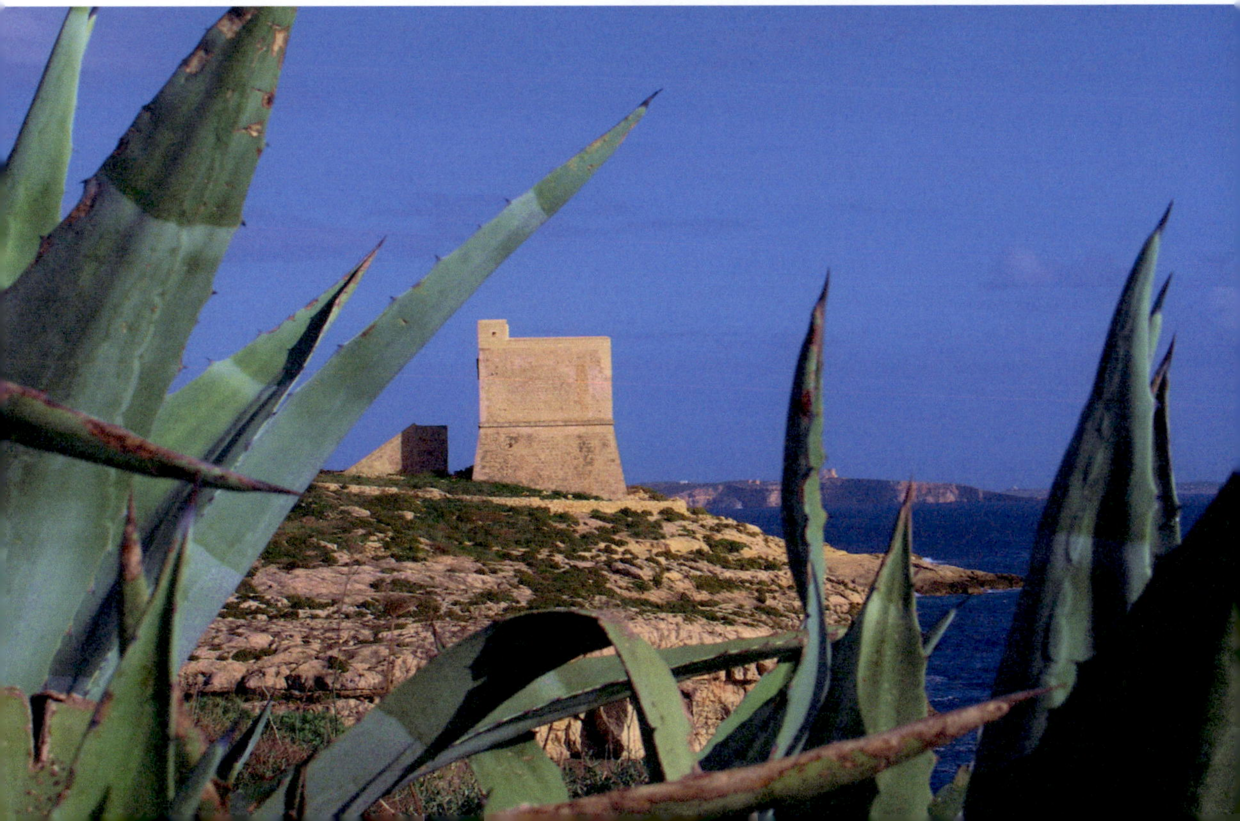

Shore dives around Gozo

The most beautiful shore dives are described below. The description enables you to locate the dive sites on your own and still ensures safe diving. In addition there are accurate descriptions for each site. In general there are three areas that are suitable for shore diving.

West of Gozo: around Dwejra Point

Dwejra Point boasts a spectacular landscape with sheer cliff faces dropping 50 m and more into the sea. Shore diving is almost impossible here, except around the Blue Hole area where the cliffs are not as

The north coast of Gozo offers excellent dive sites, if the wind is not to strong

North of Gozo: the areas around Xwieni Bay and Reqqa Point

West of Marsalforn the coastline rises steeply, and similarly underwater. At Xwieni Bay it is a predominantly sandy seabed, but further west at Reqqa Point - the seabed drops almost vertically to 20 m and more and entries become more difficult.

A final possibility to reach the sea by foot is to use the staircase at Ghasri Valley (100 steps!). Further west the cliffs are only reachable by boat. The whole area offers a multitude of good diving places. N.B. but only when there is no wind from the north.

steep and different entries offer some of the most beautiful dives of Gozo. The Inland Sea offers the additional advantage of being well protected. The spectacular landscape of the west coast is equally beautiful under water. At the weekends many local divers may be found here.

South of Gozo: from Xlendi to Hondoq Bay

Compared with the steep cliffs of the south west, the south-eastern coastline appears to be rather plain. Despite the rough shores, both Xlendi Bay and Mgarr Ix-Xini allow easy shore dives. The marine envi-

The area around Dwejra Point offers a number of diving highlights

ronment however is rather modest, mainly shallow areas of sea-grass.

Greater depths may be found by simply following the sloping seabed. Although some diving places are remarkable the south coast is only the second choice for diving. A good alternative when strong north or north-east winds make other areas inaccessible. The best places - especially the entrance to the wrecks "Xlendi", "Karwela" and "Comino Land" - may become overcrowded by divers during such periods.

The following pictograms are used to describe the main characteristics for each site.

Below: the calmer south coast

Legend

Quality of the dive site

 Excellent

 Very good

 Good

 OK

Suitable for beginner:

 Easy

 Everage

 Difficult

Underwater landscapes:

 Level, sandy seabed, no great depths

 Modest slopes, easy descent

 Drop-offs, great depths easily accessible

Weather sensitive (depending on wind direction):

 An exposed location with little protection. Highly susceptible to weather conditions

 Protected location, easy entrance even at medium surf

Other symbols:

 Caves or chimneys, don't forget lamps

 Recommended for snorkellers

 Suitable for night dives

Explanations for map:

 Route to dive site

 Parking area

 Picnic area/ rest area

 Telephone (card!)

 Snack bar

 Restaurant

 Public toilets

 Angling

 Mooring, boat traffic

 Swimming area

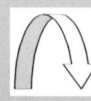 Recommended entry/ exit points

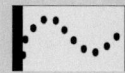 Alternative entry/ exit points

 Recommended diving route

 Off-track

Footpath

1. Xwieni Bay
[schwi-nie-baih]

A small picturesque bay approximately 2 km west of Marsalforn. A shallow sandy seabed increasing in depth far out into the bay. Covered with small channels, boulders and banks of sea-grass. Easy access even during bad weather (not possible when strong winds from the north occur). Suitable for beginner exercises and also enjoyable night dives. A safe alternative entry and exit point for diving the Double Arch an Calypso Tunnel.

Safety:
The diving site itself is not a problem, but compass bearings should be taken carefully to avoid any problems when returning to the bay. Entry and exit is only possible within the bay. On the west side, there are steep cliffs and to the east there is a shallow reef with jagged rocks. It is dangerous to exit there even in case of small waves. Pay attention to boat traffic.

The picturesque Xwieni Bay with its "White Amphora"

Route and entry directions
The journey starts in Victoria through the valley of Marsalforn via the main road directly to Marsalforn city. Keep left to Qbajjar Bay. Leave Qbajjar with the bay on your right and pass through the small settlement. Xwieni Bay is 100 m ahead. Parking areas are available beside the road. There are several entrances into the shallow water. Best of all is the slip at the bay's end, but be careful - it may be very slippery!

The dive:
The entrance into the bay via the shallow shore or the slipway is easy. The sandy ground slopes slowly into the open sea. At the beginning the seabed is between 2 and 3 m. There is a small channel at nearly 5 m that leads out into the open sea. Further channels cut their way along the seabed. Between several boulders there are areas of sand and rubble. The shoreline to both sides is rocky. A smooth sandstone wall that juts over the surface borders the

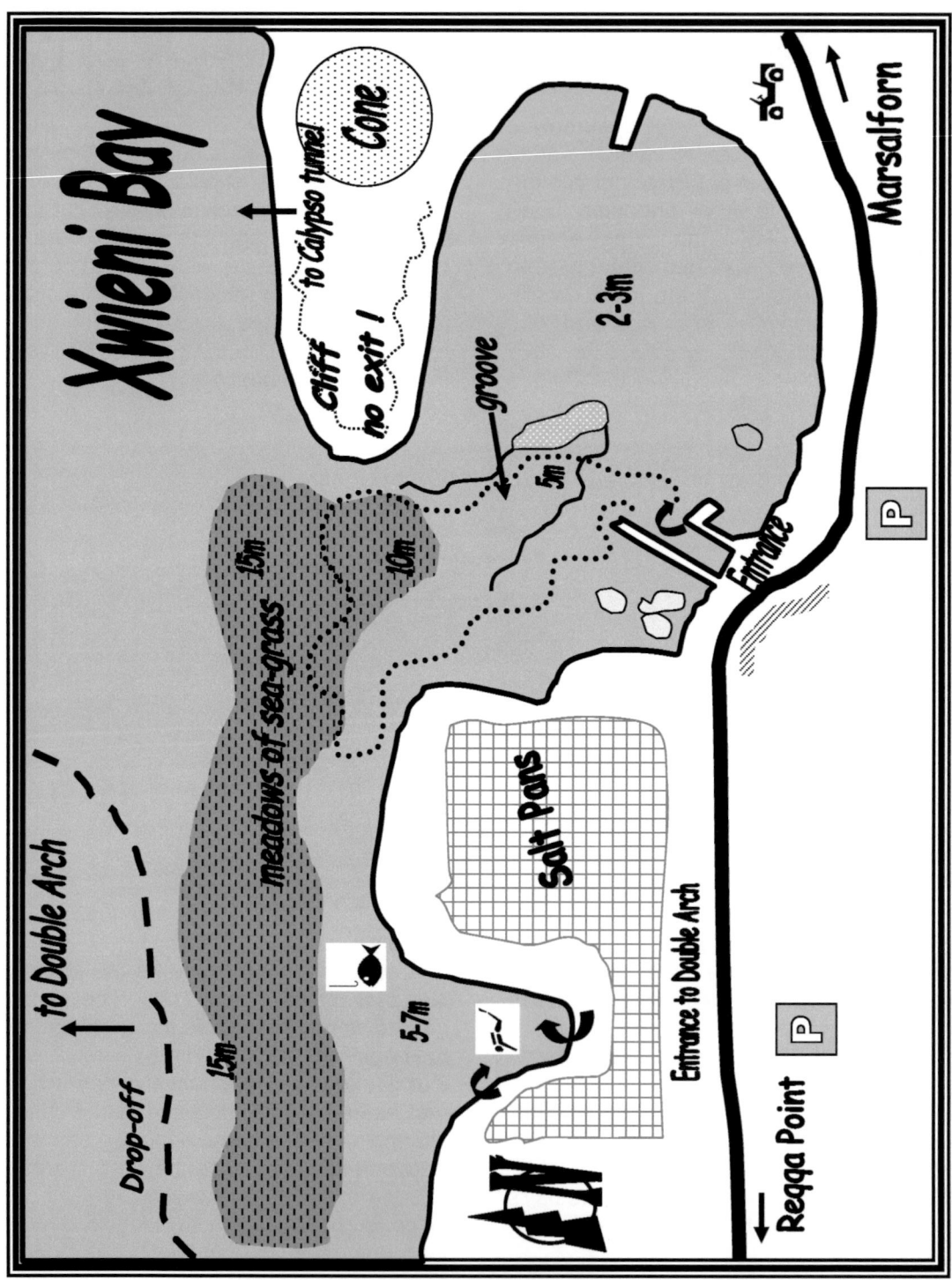

Xwieni Bay

Cone

to Calypso tunnel

Cliff no exit !

groove

5m

Entrance

2-3m

Marsalforn

P

meadows of sea-grass

15m

10m

to Double Arch

Drop-off

15m

5-7m

Salt Pans

Entrance to Double Arch

Reqqa Point

P

north-east corner of the bay. Meadows of sea-grass are scattered over the sandy seabed. An easy dive e.g. starts by entering the channel and following it a northerly direction down to 10 m. Then keep to the west. When your contents gauge indicates 100 bar ("half air") dive to the south until you reach the shore and along the southwest side of the bay back to the entrance.

If you still have sufficient air precede northwest beyond the sea-grass until you reach a drop-off. The Double Arch is located to the west. N.B.: This way requires time, so the better choice is the direct entrance to the Double Arch [-> Double Arch]. If you follow the wall to the east you will find the Calypso Tunnel, a collapsed cave with a series of arches. There you can dive up from the seabed in 35 m to a plateau in about 15 m. The easiest way to reach this place is to park the car near to the "White Amphora". Fully equipped you follow the way under the rim. Directly at the seafront you step into the water and dive straight north. You will find the drop-off after 5-7 minutes. If the course was good, you have to turn right to reach the arch after some meters rising up from the seabed at 35 m. Dive through and you'll be inside of the old cave, with its open ceiling. It is also possible to reach this place from the plateau. There you can't miss the huge opening at the bottom between the seagrass meadows. Also the shallow area between 1-4 m is nice with countless small holes and canyons.

Après diving
After the dive it is recommended to take a break at Qbajjar Bay. There are several restaurants catering for hungry and thirsty divers under parasols with a beautiful view of the sea.

2. Double Arch Reef
(Twin arches)

After crossing a large field of sea-grass one can easily attain depths of up to 35 m where one finds an impressive rock wall with two openings, which give this dive site its name. The excellent visibility, the abundance of fish and the variety in the rocky landscape make this one of the most attractive dive sites on the island.

Route and entry directions
The entrance is located 2 km north-west of Marsalforn. The route is the same way as for Xwieni Bay. There are parking facilities 100 m beyond the bay on the left hand side of the road. On the right one can see saltfields which were originally used for local salt production. Behind the salt fields there is a small bay between the cliffs, where access is relatively simple by climbing down over the rocks or alternatively by jumping approximately 2 m into the sea. Please do not step into the saltpans, because they are in use during summer time!

Safety
This site is specifically recommended for calm seas, as both the entrance and exit could otherwise present a problem. On breezy days it is safer to jump rather than risking the slippery descent and to exit via Xwieni Bay. Should you plan to exit via the twin arches entrance it is recommended to view the entry point and to take good bearings at the start of the dive.

The dive
Upon entry, head due north over the sea-

Double Arch Reef

The entrance to the Double Arch

grass fields for about 10 minutes down to 15 -17 m until you reach the edge of the drop off. Here you will find a vertical drop to approximately 30 m. In order to conserve air continue heading due north in 15 m for a further 5 minutes until you can see the wall looming before you. The wall rises vertically to within 15 m of the surface. For those who are not confident to navigate through the open water an alternative is simply to follow the rim around to the right but allow an additional 5 minutes in your dive plan.

The first arch is 2 m high and can be found at 20 m. The second arch, the larger of the two, is located immediately below it and reaches from 22 m down to the seabed at 35 m. The ceilings of both arches are covered with numerous forms of marine growth and are certainly worth viewing. The beautiful drop-offs and the giant boulders can easily make you forget the way back. Take careful note of your route and plan sufficient air and head south back over the rocky ground towards the entrance or to Xwieni Bay. If returning to Xwieni Bay head south-east away from the wall

until you reach shallow water and then use the shoreline to guide you into the bay.

Alternative dives

This entrance is also suitable for shallower and shorter dives. Neglecting the Double Arch and keeping left you will encounter meadows of sea-grass and a number of canyons and nice rivulets. By heading north at any time you always encounter the drop-off allowing you to vary your dive and depth at your leisure. The plateau narrows to the west and finishes in front of anchor reef [-> dive site 3].

Another alternative that is well worth considering is to head due north to the drop off and than follow the wall at your desired depth to the west and then return via the shallow water.

A further variation for a shorter dive is the direct way - following the coastline to the east to Xwieni Bay. It's easy to walk from this exit back to the car park.

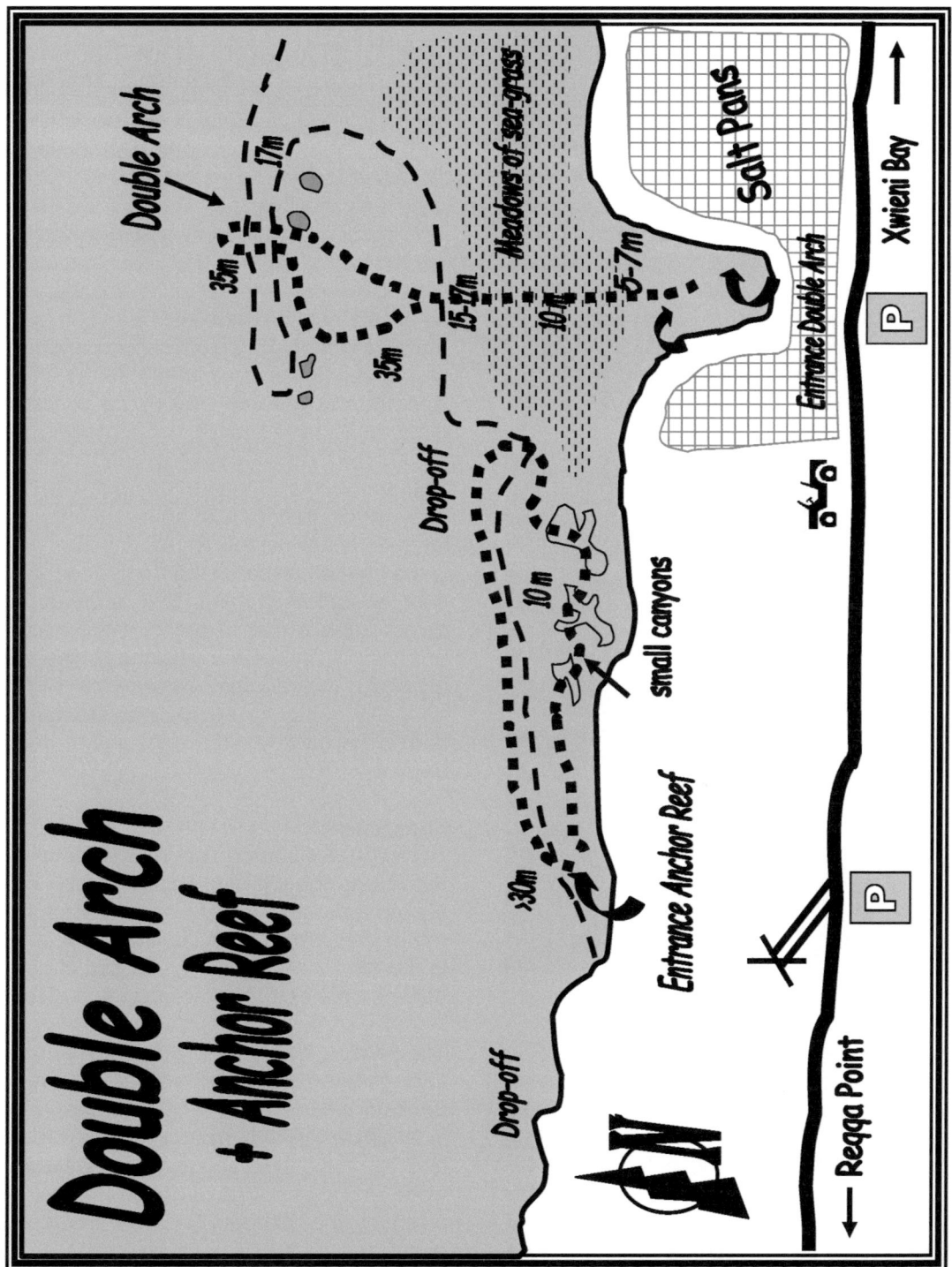

Double Arch + Anchor Reef

Double Arch

17m

35m

35m

Meadows of sea-grass

15-12m

10m

5-7m

Drop-off

10 m

small canyons

>30m

Drop-off

Entrance Anchor Reef

Entrance Double Arch

Salt Pans

Xwieni Bay

Reqqa Point

P

P

N

25

3. Anchor Reef

As you can imagine, the name is derived from an old anchor, which used to be in the reef. However, there is no point in searching for it as the elements have long since destroyed it. The entrance to Anchor Reef is between Xwieni Bay and Reqqa Point. On one side there is a drop-off and on the other there is a plain plateau with sea grass and small canyons. By heading north for just a few meters you reach the drop-off where you can observe various shoals of fish.

The coastline at the divesite Anchor Reef

Route and entry directions
The route to Anchor Reef is the same as for dive sites 1 and 2. From Victoria to Marsalforn along the coastline to Xwieni Bay, follow the road past the salt fields. After 500 m, a dirt track forks to the right running steeply down to the sea. N.B. this road is only suitable for off road 4x4 vehicles! The most practical solution is to use the car park on the main road and walk down to the water (50 m).

The access to the water is directly below the dirt track, where a small path and steps have been cut into the rocks leading to a small plateau, from where you can gain easy access. N.B. this plateau is slippery and is only suitable when the sea is calm! Alternatively you can also use a concrete platform 20 m to the left.

Safety
The biggest danger is to be swept onto the jagged rocks, particularly during the exit. Under water ownerless fishing lines present a further hazard that require the divers attention at all times. The shallow area is not critical but when you dive the drop-off, you should watch your depth gauge or computer as you may be surprised how quickly you can attain great depths.

The dive
Here you are offered two immediate alternatives: to the left, heading west, you can dive to a depth of 30 m along the wall and return the same way in shallower water, or to the right, heading east, you can choose between either a shallow or a deep dive.

The shallow dive takes you over a beautifully structured plateau with a maximum depth of between 10 -15 m. The deep dive is to follow the wall to your desired depth and returning by ascending to shallower water and then either following the wall or crossing the plateau back to the entry point.

4. Reqqa Point
[reggah-peunt]

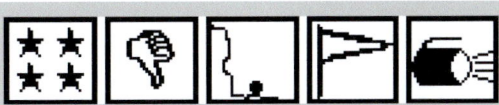

The most northerly point of Gozo is situated 3 km north-west of Marsalforn. The point stretches further north beneath the surface. This diving site is characterised by drop-offs, shelves, small caves, chimneys and, of course, an abundance of fish and may be dived at various depths.

meters to the right is a small channel that can be used as an exit. There may be a ladder available, which simplifies the exit. Generally you should plan to exit on the east side of the point, as the west is only accessible on particularly calm days. Another useful hint is to secure a rope in the channel to be used when leaving the water.

Reqqa Point - the northernmost headland of Gozo offers beautiful dives

Route and entry directions
The route to Reqqa Point is the same as described for the previous 3 dive sites. Approximately 300 m beyond the exit to Anchor Reef there is another road that is less steep (but grooves!) which leads down to the lower plateau. Follow this road for 200 m and park there. From here it is only a few steps to the water.

The easiest way into the sea is to jump from the rocks towards the east. The general practice is to use the small plateau that juts out into the sea (see photo). A few

Safety
This dive site is only recommendable for advanced divers, because the entrance and exit is difficult even with minimal waves. Watch the weather and think ahead! Changing weather conditions during the dive can make the exit extremely difficult and dangerous.

The dive
The dive starts by jumping into deep water giving the diver several alternatives:

A) Dive to the reef: By diving to 15 m and

then following the wall to the left. Between the end of the point and the reef there is a gully offering access to the west. My personal preference is to continue north-west around the reef and returning via the south side, i.e. returning to shallower water at the end of the dive. Alternatively one can dive over the reef.

The top of the reef offers a short break at about 15 m, where shoals of fish may be observed. On the northernmost side the reef reaches down into the Big Blue. Enjoy the scenery but don't be tempted to dive deeper! Diving south of the reef towards the shore there is an area scattered with giant boulders. After diving around the reef return to the point and follow the eastern wall in 10 m back to entrance.

The walls on the eastern side of the point are both interesting and beautiful and often contain surprises, particularly in shallow water. The pink growth on the overhanging cliffs is a pleasure to view during the ascent, but care should be taken to avoid the surf that can easily throw the diver against the rocks or the overhanging cliffs!

B) Instead of diving around the reef, one can alternatively dive around the end of the point and follow the coast south-west towards Billingshurst Cave. Personal air consumption and depths determine how far you go. The west side offers a vertical wall that drops to approximately 35 m.

When the sea is calm it is possible to exit at the west side of the point adjacent to the entry point. This enables divers to explore more of the west wall. If only the eastern exit is available then the diver should plan this accordingly.

C) One further alternative is to head east from the entrance along the vertical wall that drops to between 25 and 30 m. By following the wall eastwards one encounters a series of small inter-connected caves that run into a central chimney. These caves start in approximately 20 m and the chimney rises with a series of exits to within 5 m of the surface. Only experienced divers should ascend through the chimney, as it is very narrow and difficult to dive without damaging the vegetation. For others the view into the cave should be sufficient. The rest of the dive should be spent investigating the wall at various depths.

Après diving
It is nice to picnic at this scenic location.

The underwater reef at Reqqa Point

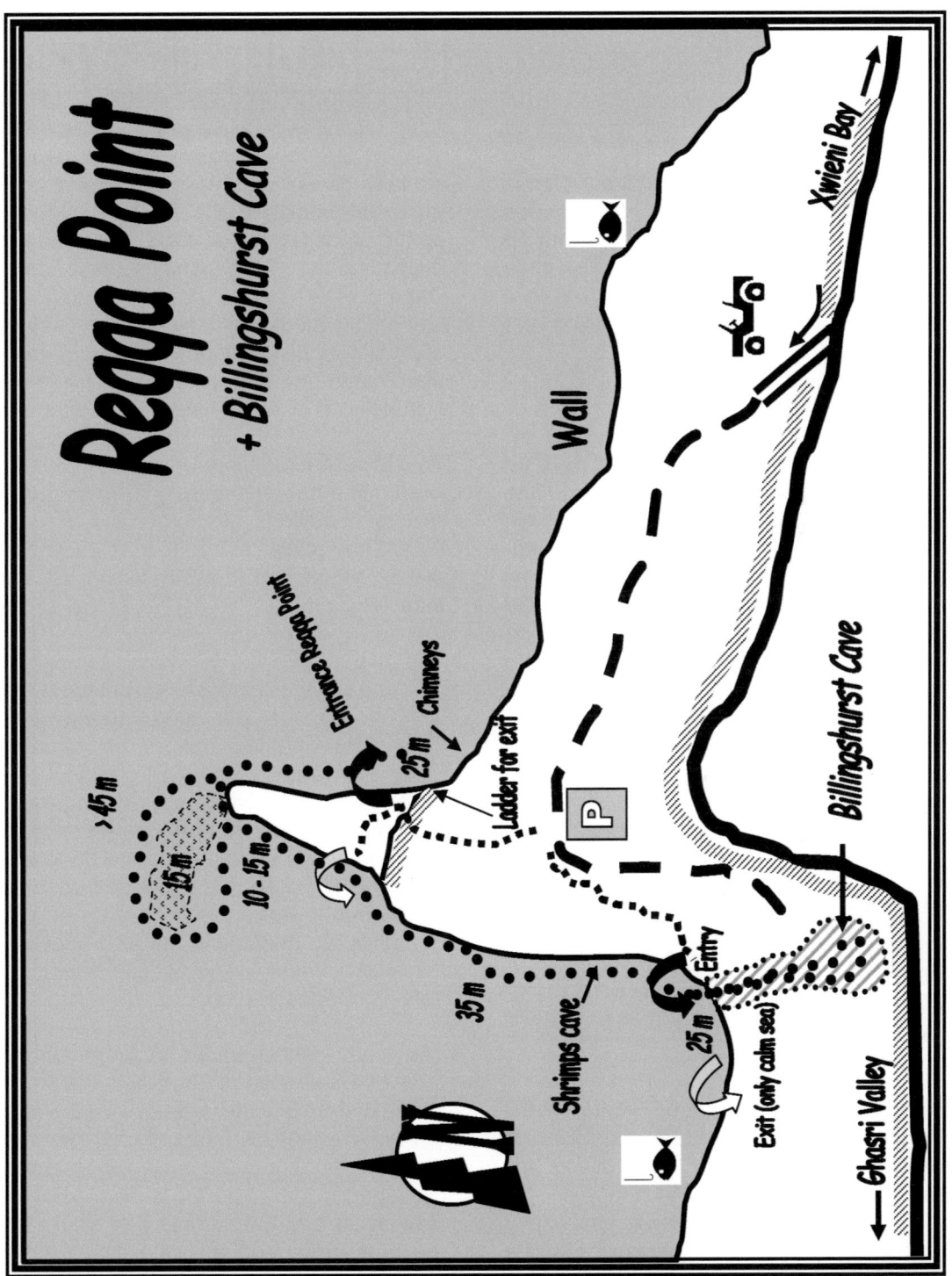

Reqqa Point
+ Billingshurst Cave

Wall

Xwieni Bay

Entrance Reqqa Point

Chinneys

>45 m

15 m

10 - 15 m.

25 m

Ladder for exit

P

35 m

Shrimps cave

Billingshurst Cave

Entry

25 m

Exit (only calm sea)

Ghasri Valley

5. Billingshurst Cave

A giant cave at Reqqa Point and easy to dive. The view from inside the cave into the open sea offers a beautiful panoramic picture. The entrance to this spacious cave is almost 20 m wide and reaches from 15 m down to the seabed at 30 m. The cave is approximately 50 m long and rises to a spectacular dome at the rear where divers can surface.

Route and entry directions
Arrival and parking is the same as for Reqqa Point, where the diver can also get into the water and swim to the cave. The better and easier choice is to jump from the rocks some 2 m above the cave entrance as this saves a lot of air and energy. For exiting you should come out at Reqqa Point. An alternative is to exit by climbing out using a small rock that juts out of the water to the left of the entrance; however this is certainly not as easy.

You can find many tube anemones in the caves

Safety
Though the cave is rather easy to dive the general safety rules for cave diving still apply. All members of the team should carry lamps. It is recommended to use a safety line when venturing deeper into the cave as there is a danger of diminished visibility due to disturbed sediment. Occasionally diving schools install ropes that make orientation much easier. Don't rely on the ropes being present. Check with the diving school when planning your dive. Depths of 30 m are possible within the cave. This should be considered in case of surfacing at the rear of the cave. Please also remember deco stops or ear pressure problems. That could hinder your return!

This dive requires careful planning and fitness. Take no unnecessary risks because rescue conditions are extremely difficult. Finally pay particular attention to buoyancy and fin movement to avoid stirring up any sediment.

The dive
The entrance to the cave is located directly where the coastline curves to the west. The giant opening cannot be missed. Enter the water by jumping from the rocks directly above the cave entrance that starts in 10 m and reaches down to the seabed at 25 m. When heading into the darkness of the cave it is recommended to look backwards towards the entrance, not only does this aid orientation but also because it offers a unique view of light effects in varying shades of blue.

The cave is shaped like a large funnel. Dive to the seabed in 25 m and follow the sandy bottom into the darkness. At the rear of the cave there is a pile of boulders that rise to within 5 m of the cave ceiling. Swim over the boulders into the cavern beyond. Now ascend to the surface and switch off the lamps for a moment. An exiting feeling!

It is pitch black and absolutely quiet. When illuminating the ceiling, you will see the dome approximately 5 m above you and the walls appear to reach into infinity.

The exit is the same way back as you entered. You should be able to see the entrance beneath you where the sunlight is shining in. Once you have left the cavern follow the ceiling to avoid going deeper and to observe the abundant growth.

Alternative 1:
Depending on your remaining air supply one can either dive or snorkel along the drop-off to the Reqqa Point exit. This takes approximately 20 minutes. The wall is well worth diving. Approximately after one third of the way back there is an entrance at 30m that opens into a small cave (called the "Shrimps Cave"). Continuing along the wall until you reach the exit as described under diving place 4.

Alternative 2:
By way of a change one can explore the coastline from the cave exit to the west.

Alternative 3:
By pre-arranging transport for pickup one can continue even further along the coast in western direction and exit at Ghasri Valley. N.B. this is approximately 900 m from Billingshurst Cave. At about half way you will pass the entrance into the Blue Dome [-> diving site 6].

6. Ghasri Valley with Cathedral
(Blue Dome) [asch-rie-wellieh]

This is a fantastic (and easy) dive into a narrow canyon that slopes down nearly 500 m where on the eastern side one encounters a cave entrance that opens into the spectacular "Blue Dome". The diver can glide into the dimly illuminated dome and surface to find a beautifully colourful panorama, especially in the afternoon when the Cathedral is lit by direct sunlight. This experience amply compensates the effort required in descending more than 100 steps fully loaded with equipment.

The canyon is located directly ahead and a steep staircase leads down to a pebbled beach where divers can dress and prepare for their dive.

Safety
In general diving Ghasri Valley is relatively simple. This dive is suitable for beginners but particular attention should be paid to both accurate air demand calculation and possible ear pressure problems. The descent via the stairs is both slippery and narrow and can sometimes be treacherous. It

Route and entry directions
The canyon can be reached via the road from Marsalforn to Reqqa Point. Do not leave the road to the cape but continue along the main road. Later, when the road turns left and heads inland, exit onto the first track to the right. At the next crossing keep left and follow this track to the end where you will find a small parking area.

is therefore recommended to make two trips to transport equipment down to the water.

The dive
The pebble beach offers an easy entrance. Head out towards the open sea. The seabed is covered with rocks; the walls to the left and right have been eroded by the

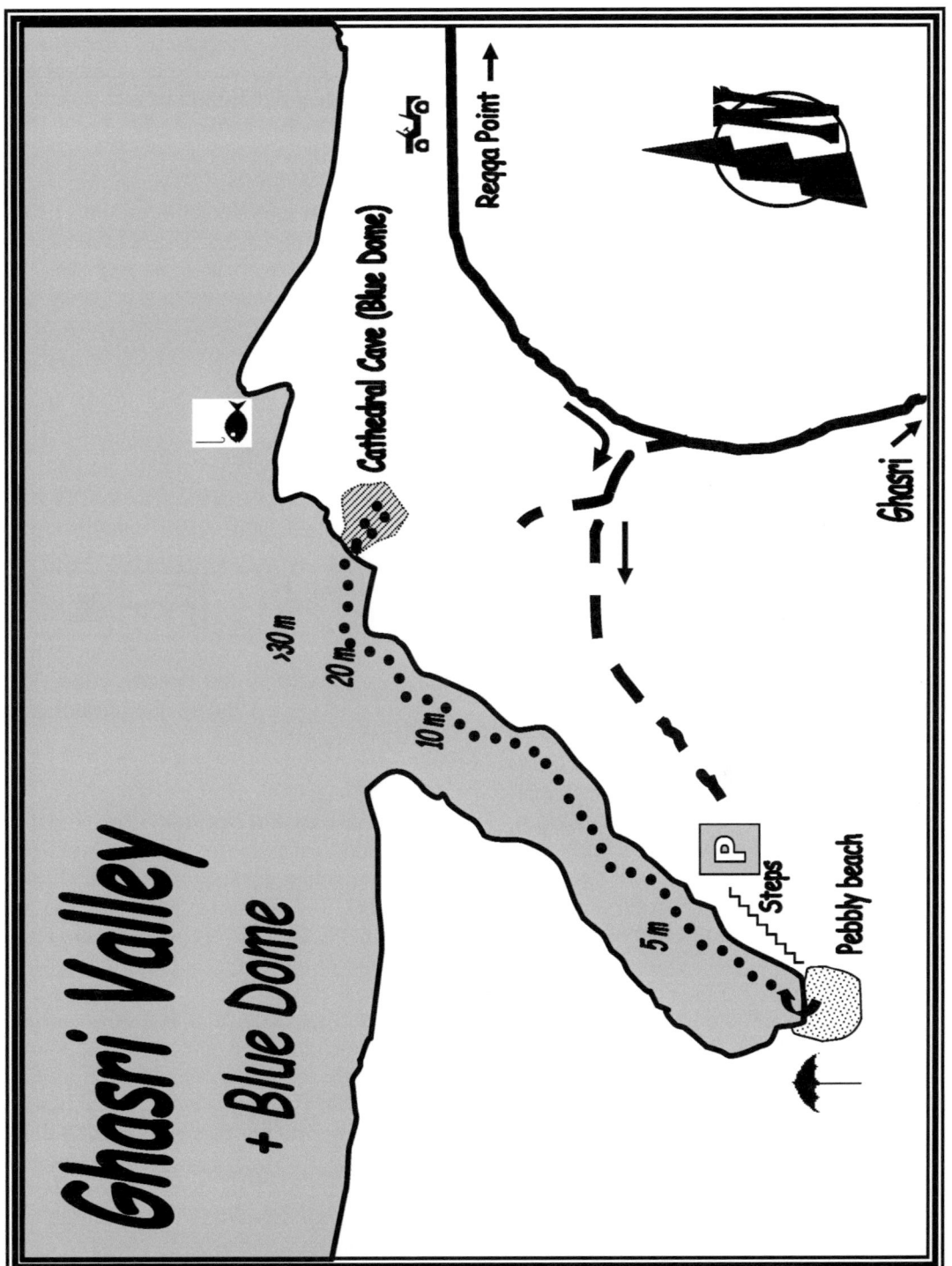

waves support an abundance of growth. The highlight of the dive, however, is the "Cathedral" which is found on the eastern side at the end of the canyon as described below. As the canyon opens into the open sea the seabed drops more steeply into an increasingly rocky landscape. It is recommended not to dive too deep and to maintain continuous contact to the wall on your right hand. Following a slight right turn you should discover the entrance into the Cathedral, a huge opening in the rock face.

The upper edge of the entrance is located approximately 5 m beneath the surface. The bottom edge lies around 15 m. When surfacing inside the dome a wonderfully lit panorama awaits the diver. This serenity can only be spoiled by loud talkative divers who drown the sounds of the gently breaking surf. After visiting the Cathedral it is well worth watching the nice rock formations around the canyon exit. Don't dive too far to the west because you can miss the canyon entrance! Towards the open sea (northern direction) the seabed drops sharply to great depths. The return journey through the canyon is a perfect way for decompression because of it is gently sloping ascent. One small disadvantage is the poor visibility following either rain or heavy surf.

Après diving
The pebbled beach is very convenient for a nice picnic. After a rest, the ascent with the heavy equipment is much easier.

7. Inland Sea

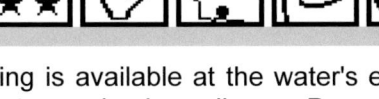

The dive starts in a small inland lake on the west coast of the island and continues through a small channel out into the open sea. The diver submerges in the cloudy lake water but the visibility improves rapidly upon entering the tunnel. The dive becomes unique with constantly changing lighting and colours ending in a dark blue horizon. Upon exiting into the open sea there are drop-offs to both sides that slope down into the depths.

Route and entry directions
Access the lake via the main road from Victoria heading west towards San Lawrenz. There turn left and follow the signs to Dwejra Point/ Azure Window. At the end of the road there is a large parking area where a smaller side road exits to the right. Turn to the right and follow the road down to the Inland Sea where limited parking is available at the water's edge. The entrance is via a slipway. Be careful: it is usually very slippery

Safety
There is a frequent boat traffic ferrying tourists through the tunnel. So you must pay particular attention to propellers and hulls overhead. For safety reasons keep to the sides in the shallow entrance area of the channel and never surface in the channel!

Divers should be aware that upon exiting the tunnel one often encounters a strong swell. Due to the sheer rock face that towers up to 50 m overhead an exit here is impossible. It is therefore absolutely essential to plan sufficient air reserves. It is equally important to ensure you are always aware of your exact position. If an ascent in open water should be necessary, keep

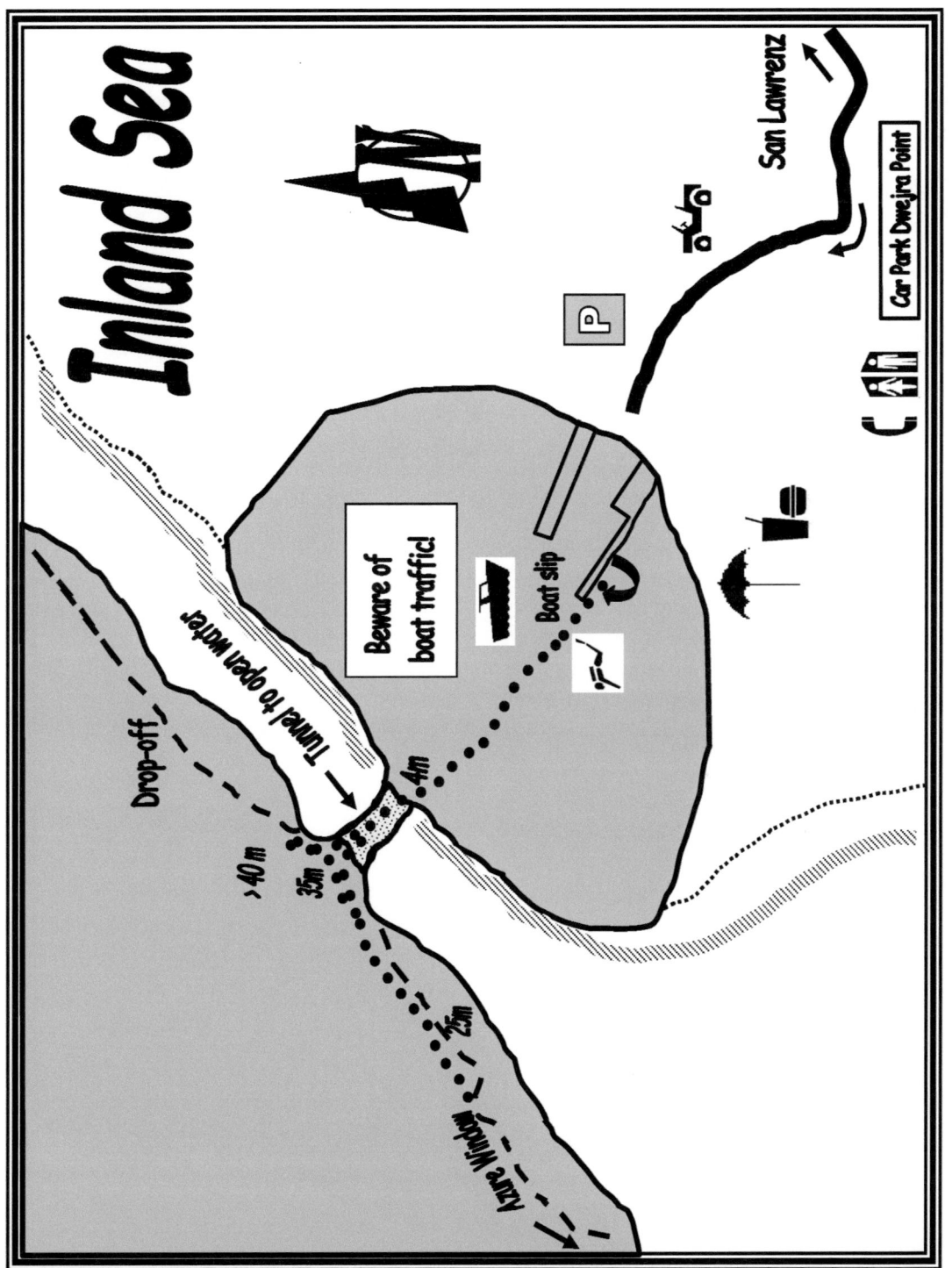

Inland Sea

San Lawrenz

Car Park Dwejra Point

P

Beware of boat traffic!

Boat slip

Tunnel to open water

Drop-off

>40 m

35m

4m

25m

Azure Window

sufficient distance to the walls. In principle it is possible to snorkel back through the channel but in view of the boat traffic and the surf it can be extremely dangerous and should be done only in emergencies!

The dive

Snorkel across the lake to the tunnel and submerge on the left hand side of the entrance. The rocky seabed is only a few meters deep. In view of poor visibility and the number of divers using this entrance, groups should pay attention that they stay together because surfacing here is a problem.

Assuming that you have overcome this first hurdle the dive can commence. During the first meters, depending on the prevailing conditions, the water may be cloudy. However, this change rapidly as you proceeds further into the tunnel. Although the visibility improves due to the absence of daylight it also becomes progressively darker, i.e. lamps are necessary! Your eyes will slowly adjust to the darkness so that you should be able to identify the light at the far end. The welcoming light increases in intensity the closer one gets to the end of the tunnel and can lead one to neglect the agreed dive plan, i.e. watch your depth because the seabed in the tunnel slopes down to 30 m.

When you reach the other end of the tunnel you should not continue out into open water but instead - depending on available air - explore the drop-offs both left and right of the exit and return through the tunnel at a shallower depth. On the way back through the tunnel take the time to investigate various shelves, small chimneys and slopes as they are well worth investigating. Before leaving the tunnel take one last glance back before entering the muddy lake water. Don't forget to listen and watch out for boat traffic!

For experienced divers only!
For experienced divers who are familiar with the diving area (Blue Hole/ Azure Window -> diving place 8) an alternative - under good weather conditions - is to exit via the Blue Hole. Upon leaving the channel the diver follows the drop-off in a westerly direction at a depth of 15 m (to avoid the surf). After 10 to 15 minutes the diver passes a broad cleft in the rock face (approximately 15 m x 20 m). One can either dive into this cleft and along the wall or cut directly across the opening and simply continue along the coastline in a westerly direction. The latter does however involve briefly losing contact to the wall.

Further along the wall one eventually reaches the Azure Window and the Blue Hole. Surf can be a problem, making an exit at this point impossible, so it is essential to check conditions before commencing the dive. The exit at the Blue Hole is only possible when the sea is calm! In view of the duration of the dive (approx. 45 minutes) this dive is only recommended for well-trained divers with sufficient air supply.

The Tunnel: "Deep Blue" awaits you!

Après diving
Nothing is more pleasurable than a break at the Inland Sea sitting under a sunshade enjoying a Hamburger or Chicken Burger and a cold beer whilst watching the other divers and the boat traffic.

8. Dwejra Point
(Blue Hole, Azure Window, Coral Cave)
[dwe-rah-point]

Dwejra Point is the most famous diving site on Gozo that boasts a beautiful landscape both above and beneath the surface. The Blue Hole is the best starting-point for various dive combinations.

Route and entry directions
The route is the same as to the Inland Sea [-> diving place 7]. When you arrive at the car park (where you will see taxis, busses and kiosks) keep left and head towards the sea and look for a parking place. From here it is only a few meters further down to the sea. The easiest entry is via the Blue

Hole just a few steps down from the car park. It is however possible to jump from the rocks at a couple of points into the open sea thereby gaining direct access to e.g. Coral Cave or Crocodile Rock [-> diving place 9] and thereby reducing an otherwise lengthy swim.

Normally the only exit is via the Blue Hole. However, when the sea is extremely calm divers may exit using a small slope that is situated on the south-west corner of the plateau running towards Crocodile Rock.

Dwejra Point

To dive the Blue Hole is one of the hightligts on a diving trip to Gozo

Safety

At this site, diving is in unprotected open water that is subject to strong winds and surf. To get an idea of what it can be like, it is recommended to visit one of the kiosks and see the postcards of the Azure Window during a storm. This dive site is difficult even under the best conditions. Emergency plans should be considered carefully when planning the dive.

One can reach all entrances with a short walk over the jagged rocks (50 - 100 m). The descent to the Blue Hole involves clambering over rocks, so boots with firm soles are necessary. One further significant point: you may encounter strong currents near Crocodile Rock.

The dive

Having clambered down to the entrance of Blue Hole the dive starts by entering a cylindrical hole that is approximately 10 m in diameter. Upon descending vertically to 7 m the wall opens on the western side offering access to the open sea. Take your bearings when leaving the hole to aid navigation on the return journey and enjoy the view as the sunlight illuminates the Blue Hole.

If you look carefully you will notice that there is a cave at the far side of the Blue Hole that is also worth exploring on your return. The seabed starts in 17 m and is covered with large boulders and slopes down very quickly into the open water. There are various possibilities to continue the dive:

A) Azure Window: Head north when leaving the Blue Hole. The Azure Window is so vast that it cannot be missed. The crystal clear water makes it easy to see the arc even from a depth of 20 m. Directly beneath the arc the water is much shallower (approx. 10 - 15 m) due to the piles of broken rocks that have accumulated there

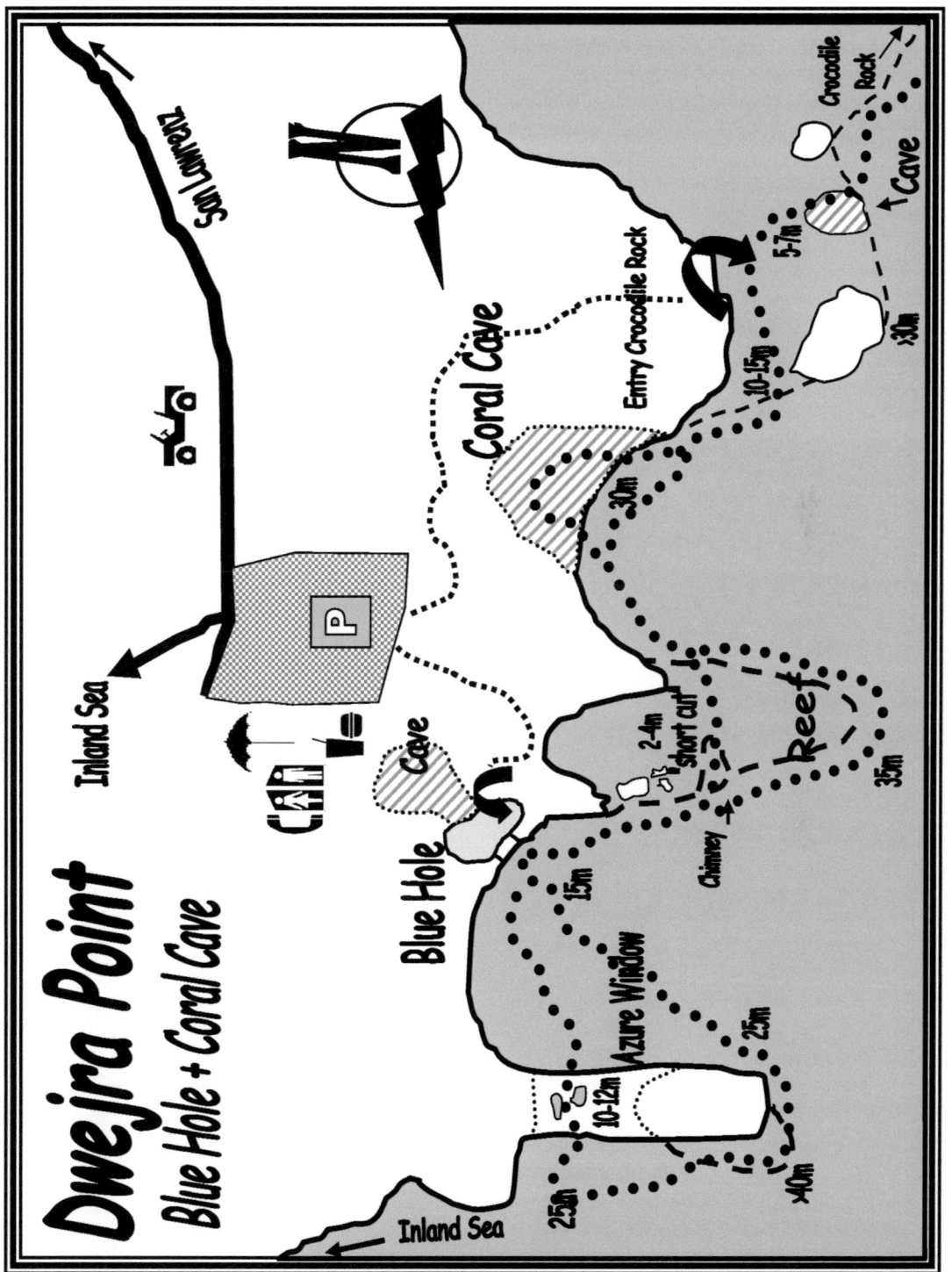

Dwejra Point
Blue Hole + Coral Cave

over the centuries. There is a small risk of rock fall; however the likelihood of being hit by a falling tourist is probably higher.

After passing the Azure Window keep left and dive around the outside pillar where various plateaus aid orientation and offer a good vantage point for fish-watching, especially for big fish. Upon encompassing the pillar, head south-east to return to the entrance of the Blue Hole. For "deep divers" it would make more sense to encompass the pillar in the opposite direction, returning to the shallower water at the end of the dive, rather than vice versa.

The tunnel at the end of the Chimney

B) The cave beneath the Blue Hole: This cave is an option to be considered at the end of the dive depending on the amount of remaining air and decompression restrictions.

The sandy seabed of the cave is found at 15 m. The ceiling starts at the entrance at 8 m and slopes down towards the rear of the cave. Please take care not to damage the numerous tubeworms. This is a spacious cave and easy to dive because its exit is always visible. Nevertheless one should observe the usual rules applicable for cave diving.

C) Another alternative is to turn left (southwest) when leaving the Blue Hole. Here the dive passes along a pretty drop-off with plenty of fish. After about 5 minutes one should find the "Chimney" that can be explored. The seabed drops off continually down to about 35 m near the point of the underwater plateau. The dive can be continued by following the wall around the point and by heading east, back towards the shore. But remember: the only exit is via the Blue Hole!

For divers who wish to shorten the route to Coral Cave or simply to avoid a deep dive I recommend to proceed as follows:

When exiting the Blue Hole in approximately 15 m, turn left and ascend along the small shelf to approximately 5 m and then head south to the other side of the point, where the wall descends vertically to 35 m. By following the drop-off to the right one rounds the point and returns to the Blue Hole exit. Shortly before reaching the exit one passes the "Chimney", which is connected to a tunnel that emerges in the shallower waters over the point. This dive may be varied in different ways.

D) By planning and executing the dive accurately the diver can reach the Coral Cave via the shortcut as described earlier. This cave is easily located when passing over the point and diving in a southern direction along the drop-off.

This cave is rather like a huge oyster shell and could easily accommodate a small house, so it is easy to dive. As one may expect the ceiling and walls of the cave are rich with plant and animal life. Please take care of your buoyancy and be with this fragile and unique habitat careful! The view from inside the cave out into the open sea is quite impressive. Don't forget to watch your depth and bottom time and remember that you have a long way back.

Après diving
There is a snack bar beside the car park where one can sit under sunshades and enjoy the beautiful view. However, it is usually full of tourists. N.B. this is one of the best places on Gozo to observe the sunset, especially as most of the tourists have usually left by then.

9. Crocodile Rock

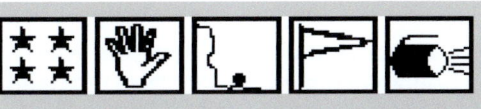

There are a number of other diving sites at Dwejra Point besides Blue Hole, Azure Window or the Inland Sea. In front of the western cape there is a little rock that appears from the shore to look like a crocodile. This site offers some marvellous drop-offs and plenty of fish as well as large shoals of barracudas. There are also a few clefts and small caves that are worth exploring

Route and entry directions
The route is the same as for diving sites 7 and 8. Try to park in the south-west corner of the car park to reduce the distance to the entry point, which is along a footpath to the most south-westerly point. The dive starts opposite the large rock with a 2-3 m jump into 5 m of water. The walk to the entry point runs over jagged rocks, so it is recommended to do a dry run first before doing it with heavy equipment.

Exits here are only possible when the sea is extremely calm and divers can climb out over some of the lower (jagged!) rocks. However, the prevailing conditions make this seldom possible. The normal exit is via the Blue Hole.

Safety
The exit via the rocks is difficult at any time and certainly not suitable for any emergency activities. The dive should be planned carefully, with particular consideration for the long return journey to the Blue Hole exit. Furthermore one may encounter strong currents beyond the Crocodile Rock.

N.B. it is important to remember that even if air supplies are running low and one decides to snorkel to conserve air, one still needs sufficient air for the exit through the Blue Hole. This dive is only suitable for experienced divers in good physical shape.

Crocodile Rock

<u>The dive</u>

It is preferable to enter the water by jumping from the rocks and then gliding down to a plateau at 7 m. From there the best way to dive is straight ahead to the drop-off between the two rocks (the small and the big bear). Once you reach the wall keep left. Directly beneath the smaller rock the wall turns to the south-west.

At this point there is a cave entrance at approximately 20 m. After exploring this cave the diver can then follow the wall. At the bottom of the drop off in 35 m the seabed is covered with boulders and it slopes down and out into the open sea.

Divers wishing to explore the deep area beneath the cave should be aware that their air supply would be insufficient to also reach Crocodile Rocks reef cape. Extended dives at this site can only be recommended when it is calm and the exit is possible via the entry point. From the cave follow the wall at any depth until it turns to the south-east. This is immediately below the "Crocodile". Ascend and continue in a north-eastern direction across the plateau. After only a few meters one can find a small "amphitheatre" eroded in the rock. This place is also famous for encountering lots of barracudas. If you intend to exit at the Blue Hole then it is necessary to plan the dive slightly differently. Taking the length of the dive into account it is important to avoid depths in excess of 25 m. One should first dive the cave and then follow the wall to the point beneath Crocodile Rock as described above.

There are a number of large clefts in the rock face that can be explored. After encompassing the "Crocodile" one can start the long return journey back to the Blue Hole. The shortest route is to follow the wall back at a shallower (10 - 15 m) depth, passing the smaller rock. Continue in a northern direction past the entry point towards the larger rock. Both rocks can be easily seen from under water just by looking up to the surface.

Beyond the larger rock the wall turns towards the coastline. It is recommended to ascend to approximately 10 m where the top of the wall borders the plateau and then to head north-east towards the giant entrance of the Coral Cave. From there follow the way back to the Blue Hole as described in diving site 8. This is a nice long dive but a large tank is almost compulsory.

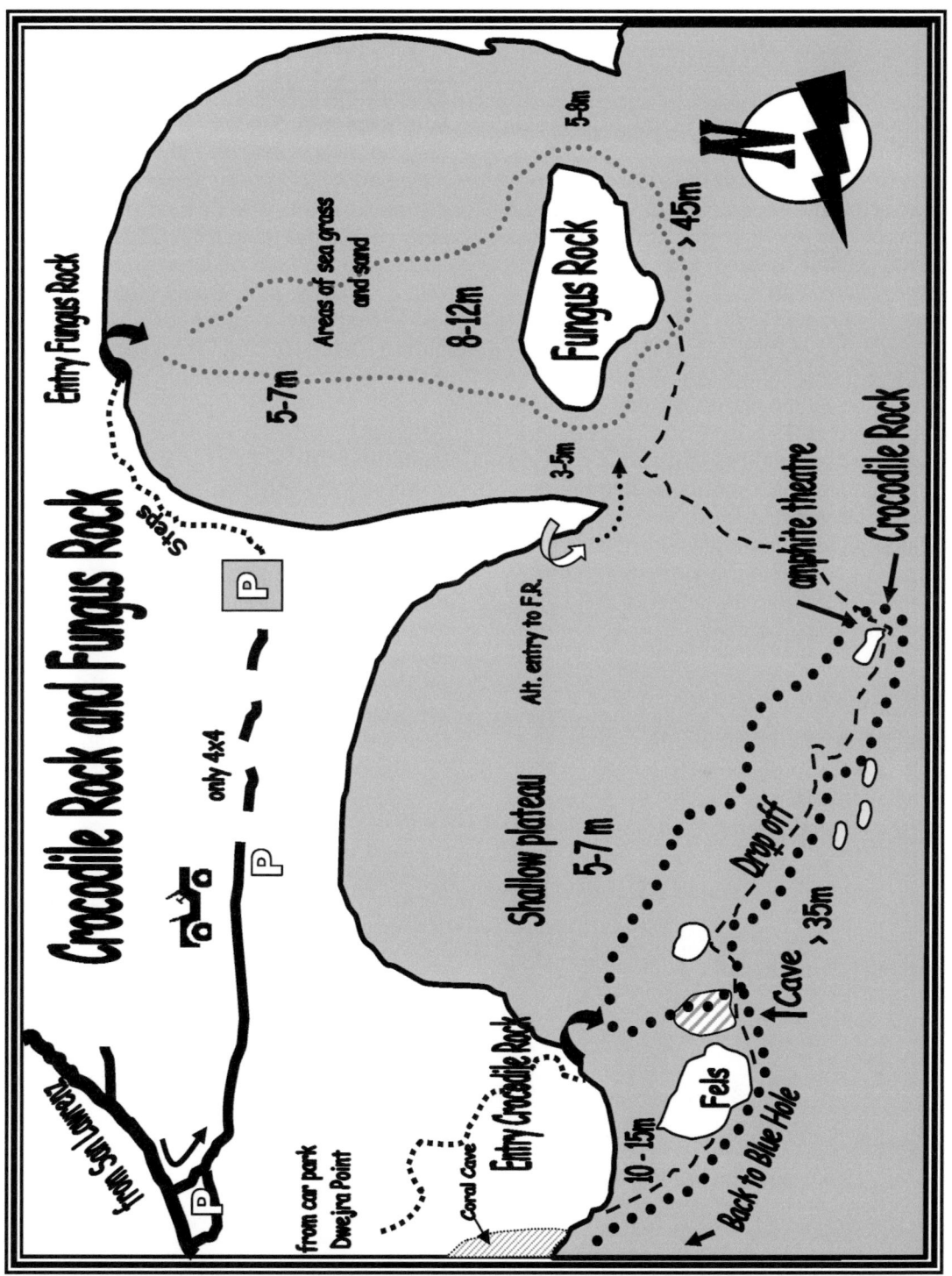

10. Fungus Rock

Fungus rock is located south of Dwejra Point in the centre of the entrance to Dwejra Bay. On the seaward side of the rock there are some spectacular drop-offs and it is renowned for the abundance of fish. Divers without a boat who don't mind a lengthy swim can easily snorkel out to the rock.

Roue and entry directions
The route is the same as for the other dives around Dwejra Point. Before reaching the main parking area turn left to one of the smaller exits and follow it to the southern most parking area, where the track for normal vehicles ends. However, with a jeep it is possible to drive closer to the shoreline. The entry to the water is done via a staircase and a boat slip.

Safety
Similar to the other diving sites around Dwejra Point the great depths that are possible always present a potential risk. In case of emergency, the rescue process is both long and difficult. This place should only be dived when the sea is calm. One may encounter strong waves and surf at the exits of the bay and on the seaward side of the Fungus Rock. The entrance and exit point also becomes more difficult with increasing surf. Boats that frequently use the bay as an anchoring place are a further risk. Strong currents may be encountered in front of Fungus Rock.

The dive
Once you are suited up follow the steps down into the bay and enter the water via the boat slip. The most direct route to the rock is about 400 m long and should be snorkelled to conserve air. The bay is between 7 to 12 m deep with a sandy bottom and sea-grass meadows. The most beautiful spots around Fungus Rock are located on the south-west side. It is best to start the dive in the southern bay exit, since from here one can quickly get to the drop-off which reaches down to 45 m and more. In some places you will find small plateaus

that drop in steps. Also a small cave may be found at a depth of about 15 m. Giant rocks are scattered over the seabed. Following the wall along the seaward side of Fungus Rock it will become increasingly shallower as one nears the northern entrance to the bay (5 m). For this reason it is

important to do any necessary decompression stops whilst still on the westward, seaward side of the rock. The sheltered side of the rock may be dived but it is not as interesting as the seaward side.

11. Xlendi Bay
[schlendi-bäih]

On the northwest coast of Gozo is a small tourist village called Xlendi. A collection of hotels, bars, restaurants and diving schools are huddled along the seafront of the fjord like bay. In earlier times the Romans used the bay as a winter harbour.

These days it is dominated by tourists pursuing all kinds of water sports. Divers are more interested in the small reef and a tunnel which are located in the mouth of the bay. Especially the shallow water makes this site suitable for beginners.

Route and entry directions
Coming from Victoria, Xlendi is impossible to miss. Just follow the signposts. In Xlendi follow the road along the south side of the bay. The road then climbs and in the first sharp left-hand curve you will find limited parking facilities on your right. From here there are two staircases running down to the water. On the seafront there are platforms with ladders which make the entrance and exit easy.

Safety
The bay is very shallow and is used for anchoring a lot of boats. Therefore boat traffic presents the biggest danger. Caution is required when swimming or surfacing. A network of anchor lines litters the bay and there is a possible danger to get caught in them. A small tunnel, approxima-

tely 30 m long, can be found on the northern shore of the bay. Diving through the tunnel is possible, but again should be done with care. It is rumoured that wastewater is occasionally discharged into the bay (during heavy rainfalls!). This pollution could pose a potential health threat. Some diving schools use the bay whereas others avoid it on principle.

The dive
An easy dive is to start on the south shore and to head north across the bay, where the seabed varies between 6 - 8 m. The northern side of the bay is an almost vertical wall that one should follow around to the left (southwest) towards the exit of the bay. The entrance to the Xlendi Cave is easily found in approximately 3 m. The cave (in reality a tunnel that cuts through the point) is not very spacious at the beginning but as one progresses it widens.

Xlendi Bay

The busting seafront of Xlendi Bay

At the far end it resembles a gorge where it is possible to surface. This site is especially suitable for beginners to experience cave diving conditions. Nevertheless the channel is an adventure for advanced divers, too. The fascinating light conditions and the opulent growth on the walls make this a pleasure for all divers. Upon exiting in approximately 6 m the diver should keep left and follow the wall to the end of the point and back into the bay.

Alternatively one may continue to head south over the rocky seabed for about 5 minutes to the Xlendi Reef, which reaches up from 20 m to the surface. When returning keep the wall to your left and head back into the bay until the seabed is approximately 8 m. Then cut across to the starting point on the south shore.

Variations of the dive

The narrow bay found to the left of the starting point on the south shore is particularly suitable for beginners. Seagrass meadows and small rocks offer an interesting terrain to discover the marine world with depths of less than 10 m. N.B. observe the prohibited zone beneath the ancient guard tower at the bay's exit.

Après diving

This pleasant bay presents a number of restaurants and cafes for a welcome break after the dive. The restaurants that are close to the parking area offer a nice view at sunset.

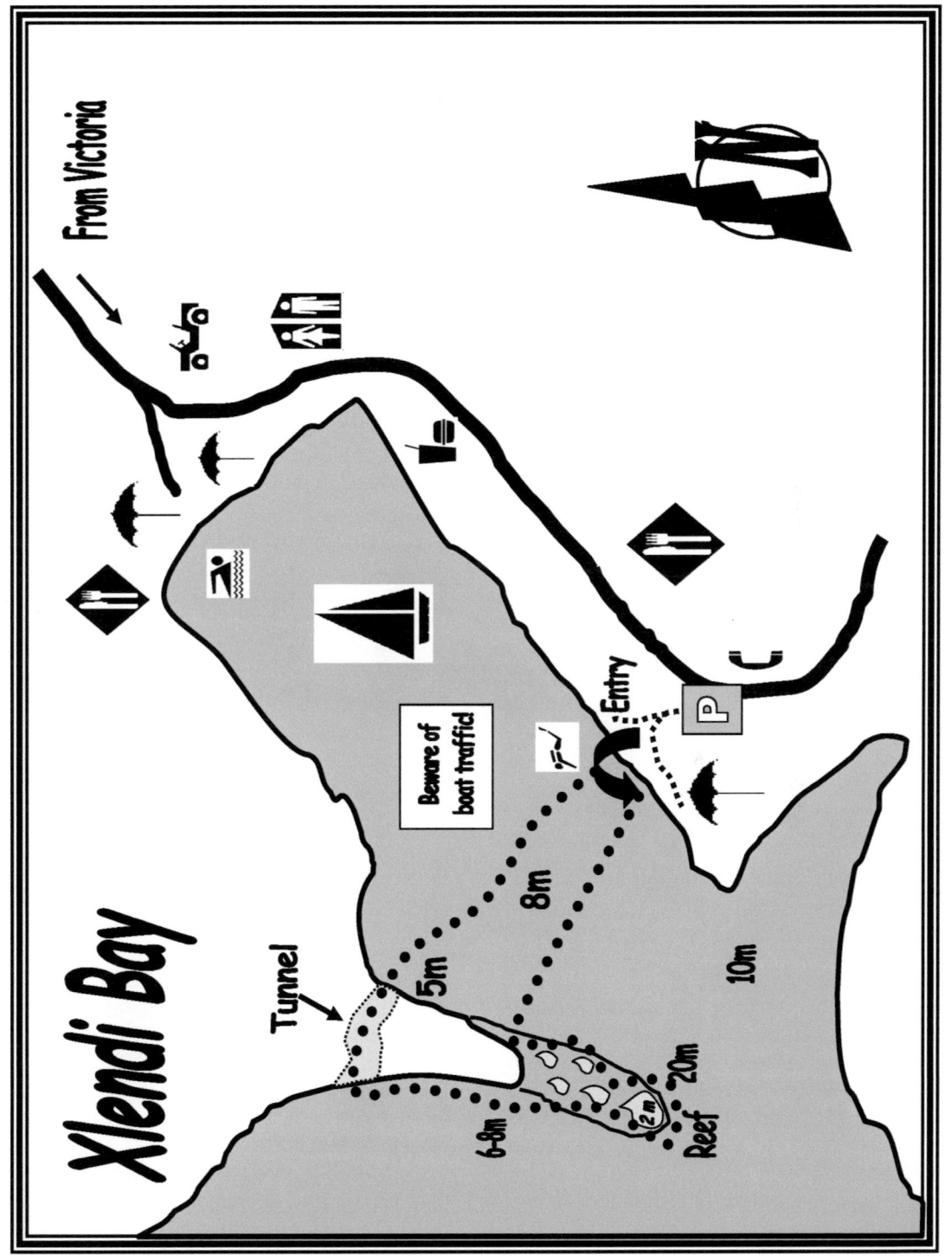

12. Ta'Cenc (Il Kantra)
and Fessej Rock
[Ta-schensch / Fess-saih-rock]

The Ta'Cenc cliffs are situated on the south coast west of the entrance to the canyon of Mgarr Ix-Xini (-> diving place 13). This popular site is protected from north-west winds, which regularly inhibit diving along the western and northern coastline. This site offers a lot of possibilities for both beginners and advanced divers: a sandy seabed that is teeming with marine life, drop-offs, small caves and the mighty Fessej Rock that reaches down to almost 50 m. Because the entrance to the dive site is situated at a private area, diving can be limited occasionally.

sign for "Il Kantra/ Snack Bar" (the sign is only present during the holiday season). It is almost impossible to take the wrong road, because barriers block the side roads. The road finishes in a dead-end where you can turn your car. Do not park here but turn and look for a parking space on the right hand side of the road.

Directly beneath the parking area is a small restaurant, which belongs to the Ta'-Cenc Hotel. Steps lead down to a concrete platform where the diver can jump into the water. A ladder is usually hanging in

Some steps leads you to the water

Route and entry directions
Follow directions from Victoria to Sannat. Turn left past the church and continue through the village in a south-eastern direction. At the next fork keep left and continue for approximately 100 m where you will enter private property. The road continues through a series of bends down to the sea. Just before the road ends, there is a small turn-off to the right. Follow the

the water during opening hours, which makes exiting easy. Out of business hours, one must exit by climbing over the rocks.

It should be mentioned that due to increasing diving activities the owner and hotel guests feel disturbed. So this place should be preferably dived in the early morning (before 10 am) or late afternoon (after 4 pm). Otherwise it could be that access is

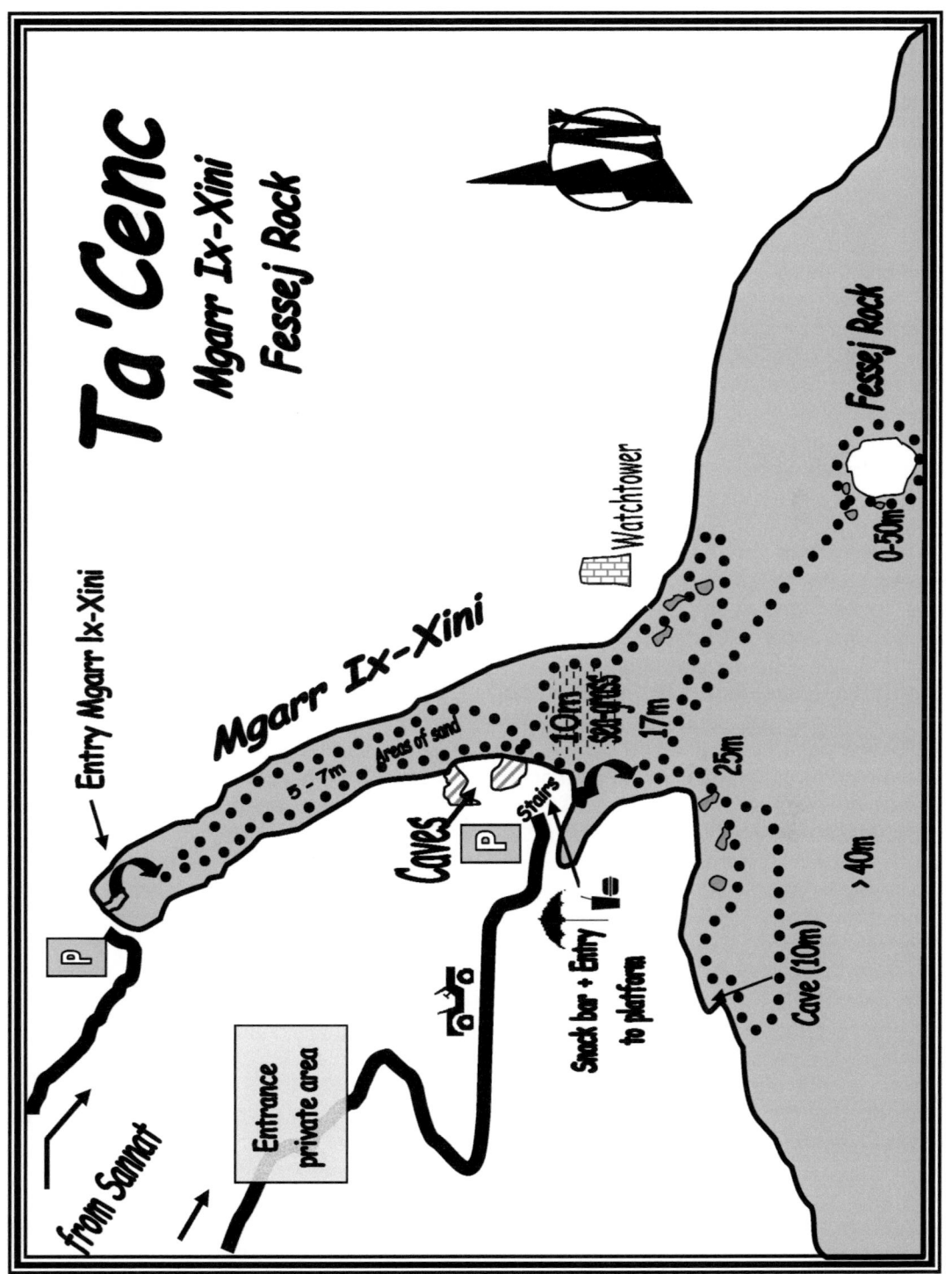

prohibited. This is a private property and divers should take this into consideration. It would be courteous to enquire at the hotel reception beforehand.

Safety
This diving site has no particular dangers, but the caves are rather narrow so the diver should dive them with necessary caution. Generally, unlike the dive sites on the northern and western coasts, the sea-bed slopes down gently towards the open sea. Diving to Fessej Rock however is only suitable for advanced divers with sufficient physical condition. It is a long distance to the rock and occasionally one may encounter currents.

The dive
This area offers various dive possibilities. Starting from the platform one can either dive to the right along the coastline and around the cape or to the left across the bay and along the eastern shoreline. Both shores have drop-offs with small caves and chimneys and scattered rocks. The walls are not as steep as found on the western or northern coastline; depths of 40 m can be reached relatively quickly, but rocky terrain changes to a rather boring sandy seabed. It is most interesting between depths of 10 - 30 m. On the shallow sandy ground at the bay exit the diver finds large meadows of sea-grass at approximately 10 m. This area should be given particular attention as usually one may discover sand eel, ray, gurnard, plaice and with a little luck pipefish and even seahorses. Diving on the left hand side of the bay towards the canyon one discovers two caves. The entrance to the first cave stretches from the seabed to just below the surface and reaches back 10 to 15 m into the rock. The second is approximately 50 m further along. It is by comparison consider-

ably smaller but twists and turns its path deeper into the rock. At the end of the dive it is worth investigating the shallow area around the entry point as the walls and rocks harbour a variety of marine life.

Another alternative is to dive straight ahead from the entry point towards Fessej Rock. This is only recommended for the advanced diver who is prepared for the 400 m swim that is necessary to merely get to the rock. To conserve air it is recommended to dive at a depth of 5 m following a pre-determined compass bearing. It is a great feeling to suddenly see the rock appearing out of the gloom ahead of you. For those who don't trust their orientation skills or who wish to use their entire air supply for exploring the rock, they can snorkel the whole way, but watch out for boat traffic! The rock grows like a pillar from the sandy seabed at 50 m and can be circled at various depths whilst spiralling towards the surface. There are numerous boulders located around the base.

The drop-offs give home to an abundance of fish life. There is also a good chance to find larger fish e.g. grouper, barracuda and tuna. The walls of the rock are rich in vegetation and marine life, so even the smallest of holes or crevices may contain surprises. At the end of the dive one should return via the most direct route to the exit point. N.B. check if there is any current before the dive. If necessary avoid any risk and only dive along the coastline.

Après diving
Take advantage of the sunshade, the drinks and the beautiful view from the nearby restaurant. Snacks are also available for hungry divers. A snack or a drink at the beach bar can be seen as compensation for the use of their premises.

13. Mgarr Ix-Xini
   [Im-Scharr-ih-schini]

In former times pirates used this gorge-like canyon as a hideaway. Later it became a protected harbour for the knights of Malta. Today, the bay with its sandy seabed and steep walls is very convenient for night dives. During daytime it is especially attractive for beginners. A great number of species can be observed, living on or below the sandy bottom. As already described, at the canyon exit there are two caves, which can be dived quite easily.

and holds no particular dangers, assuming care is taken to observe the occasional boat traffic. This site is ideal for night dives and even in darkness it is difficult to lose your way. Even the caves present no particular risk assuming the dive is planned properly. A word of warning: don't dive too far into the first cave because it becomes increasingly narrow.

Route and entry directions
The bay is reached via Victoria and Sannat. In Sannat keep left in front of the church (same as to Ta'Cenc) and continue through the town. Look out for a small sharp turning to the left that leads down a steep hill to Xewkija. Follow this road down through the valley and at the deepest point (shortly before Xewkija) you should see a sign to Mgarr Ix-Xini. Turn right on to this small road and follow it for approximately 2 km. At the end of the road there is a very sharp left-hand curve which is followed by a 20% descent directly to the bay. There are parking facilities for vehicles. Access to the sea is easy using the slipway. N.B. very slippery!

Safety
The maximum depth in the bay is 10 m

The dive
After snorkelling through the shallow area it is best to start the dive by following the steep wall on one side of the canyon to the mouth of the bay. From here swim across to the opposite side and then head back along the wall to the starting point. The two caves are located on the western shoreline close to the bay's exit. Focus your attention on the sandy seabed where you will find plenty of gurnard and plaice. For night dives it is recommended to illuminate the entrance as the only other sources of light are the stars.

Après diving
There is a small restaurant in the bay. The kind owners prepare delicate seafood and are happy to arrange barbeque for larger groups by announcement.

14. Xatt l-Ahmar (Mellieha Point) with wrecks Xlendi, Karwela, Comino Land [Schatt-la-mahr]

Close to the harbour of Mgarr is the idyllic Mellieha Bay directly beneath Fort Chambray. This bay offers easy entrance to shallow water. Various other entrances are located along the shoreline to the west. This area is suitable for both beginners and experienced divers and offers an alternative to Ta'Cenc in case of north-west winds.

prohibited to dive inside. Get an impression from respectful distance. Beside the hull you can find a car wreck. The sinking of the other two wrecks was supported with subsidies of the EU and worked much better. The hulls of the ships are lying between 20 - 35 m and are prepared to dive (carefully) inside.

The idyllic Melieha Bay on the Red Coast (Xatt l-Ahmar)

For some years past three additional attractions were prepared for advanced divers: The wreck of the car ferry "Xlendi" was sunk in 1999, followed be the vessels of the "MV Karwela" and the "MV Comino Land" in the summer of 2006. Unfortunately the "sinking" of the "Xlendi" did not go as planned as it drifted away from the designated site and sank funnel down in 40 m of water. Many superstructures are now stuck in the sand or have simply been destroyed by the weight of the ferry. ATTENTION: after 10 years lying on the seabed, this wreck is very unstable, so it is

Route and entry directions
Start from Victoria and head towards Mgarr. After crossing the only traffic light on Gozo you first pass the Gozo-Heliport and finally reach the village Ghanjsielem. Continue through the village and after approximately 500 m one passes a building with a large sign "Gozo-Press". Turn right immediately behind this building onto the road named "Triq Ta Cordina". Follow this road and turn left at the second branch, onto a bumpy track, which runs between fields down to the sea. Continue from here eastwards along the coastal

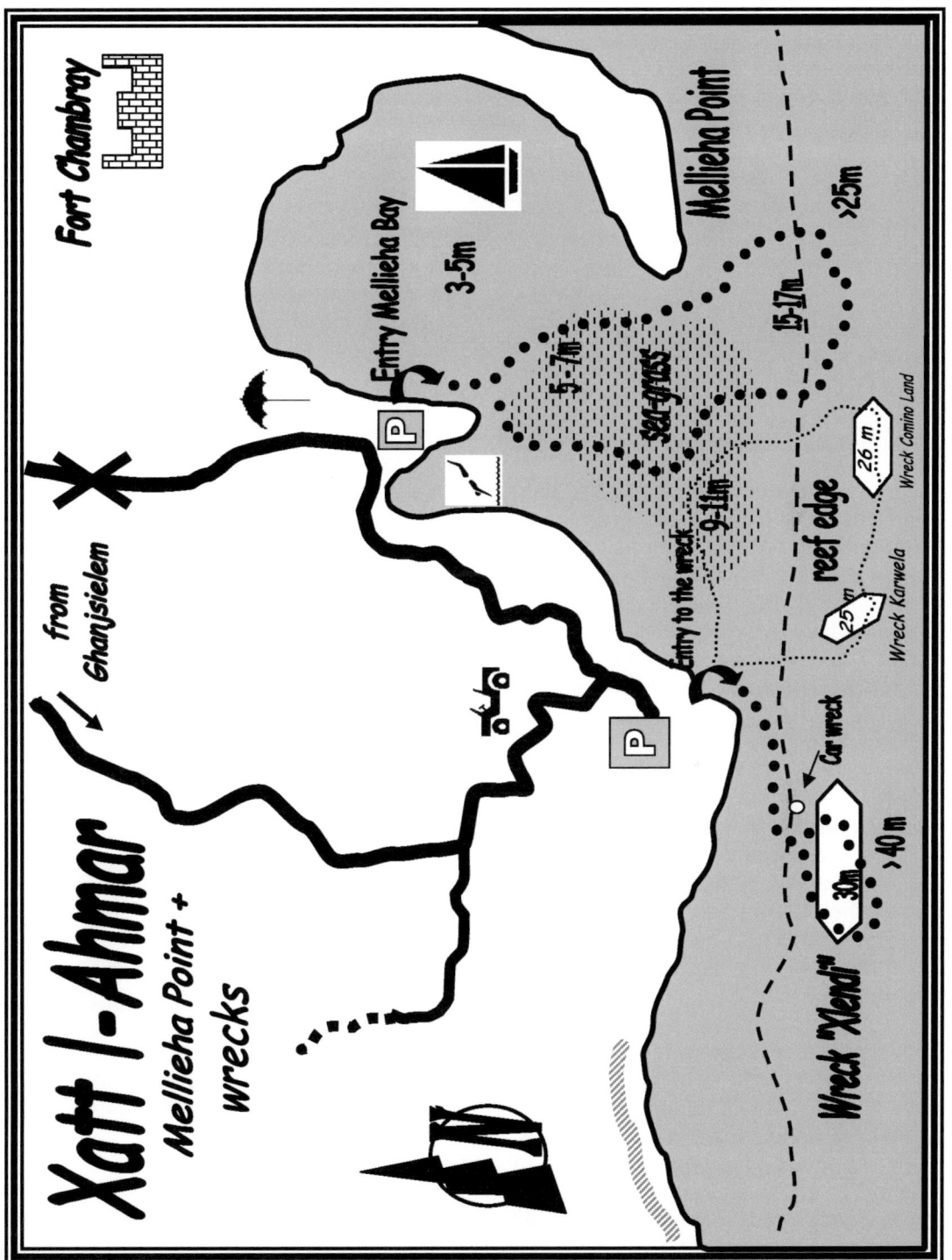

Xatt l-Ahmar
Mellieha Point + wrecks

Fort Chambray

from Ghanjsielem

Entry Mellieha Bay

3-5m

Mellieha Point

5-7m

Sea-grass

9-11m

15-17m

>25m

reef edge

Wreck Comino Land

26 m

Wreck Karwela

25 m

Entry to the wreck

Car wreck

30m

>40 m

Wreck "Xlendi"

53

track to Mellieha Bay, where you will find limited parking space. At the bay the diver can jump into the sea at several places. N.B. the concrete platforms and the boat slip are extremely slippery!

To get to the wreck site follow the same route down the bumpy track between the fields and turn right as soon as you reach the coast. There is a new parking area prepared for the divers beside the track. A footpath leads over the rocks down to the water. The easiest access is to jump from the rocks. Signs-boards with the lettering "DIVING WRECKS" makes it nearly impossible to miss the way to this place.

Safety
This region has in principle no dangers. Close to the shore it is shallow and there are no steep drop-offs. Of course further out depths of 40 m and more are attainable. Pay attention to occasional boat traffic, in particular to boats using the bay for anchoring.

Diving on the wrecks is more risky. The seabed at this area begins at 30 m and goes down to over 40 m, so diving is hardly possible without making decompression stops. As mentioned before diving on the "Xlendi" is extremely dangerous. To dive inside of this wreck is prohibited. But also be careful while diving the other wrecks. In

principle diving into these hulls is possible, but carries all the risks attributed to wreck diving. Therefore only advanced divers should do this dive. Beginners should contend themselves to viewing the hulls from above only!

Variation of the dive
Within Mellieha Bay it is very shallow with a maximum depth of 5 m. Outside the bay it slowly becomes deeper. In the area beyond the mouth of the bay the diver finds small rocks and meadows of seagrass. Upon closer inspection one usually finds not only shrimps but also octopus and a lot of small fish. To reach depths in excess of 10 m it is necessary to dive further south beyond the plateau where the sandy seabed slowly slopes into the depths.

A) It is possible to dive the same area starting from the "wreck entrance" which is located 300 m to the west. The rocks around this entrance are slightly larger, covered with various marine growths and offer a number of small holes. It is also possible to explore the coastline further westwards.

B) Wreck dive (for advanced divers only): To locate the "Xlendi" divers should follow the shoreline westwards from the entrance B) at a depth of about 15 m. The bright hull of the former ferry should be visible on the sloping sandy seabed running parallel to the coastline. The first contact with the keel is made at around 30 m. The ferry has screw propellers at both ends to aid manoeuvrability - a feature typical for ferries. By descending from the keel down

The MV Karwela

the side of the ship and superstructures one reaches the sandy seabed in about 42 m. Please hold respectful distance to the unstable hull and don't dive inside! In view of the depths and bottom times involved it is necessary to observe all deco-stops before returning to the surface.

C) Karwela and Comino Land: Because of the depth, each wreck should be dived seperately. So there is enough time to discover all the sights of the wrecks. You also start at entrance b). When following a compass bearing of 200 degrees you will find a drop off. Dive ahead into the open water and you'll reach the Karwela soon. After a short while the bow of the wreck appears. The 50 m long patrol boat lays

horizontally on the sandy bottom. The upper deck is situated at about 30 m. The mast produdes to the surface. On the backward board an old Volkswagen is placed.

If you like to visit the other wreck at the same dive, rise up to 20 m and take a bearing of 80 degrees. After 2-3 minutes you will reach the Comino Land, which was an excursion boat in former times. To explore the boat more thuroughly, you have to des-

VW-beetle on deck of the MV Karwela

cend again to at least 30 meters. Better to do this in a second dive! To go back ascend to 15 m and dive with a northwest-course back to the coastline. The shallows plateau is perfect to spend the - eventually needed - decompression time

Après diving
The Mellieha Bay is a nice place for a break and to enjoy the scenery. As there are no snack bars available it is recommended to take your own food along or even do as the locals do and have a barbecue down at the water.

15. Hondoq Bay
[Honn-dock-bay]

The south-east coast of Gozo is not very attractive for divers; however under certain weather conditions (wind from north or west) this bay is protected and offers an alternative to Mellieha Bay or Mgarr Ix-Xixi. One dives in a small sandy bay directly opposite Comino. The site is especially popular for beginners to gain their first diving experiences and for night dives.

The dive
A great advantage at this site is the uncomplicated entrance either via the beach or by a jump from the quay. One should not expect anything special during the dive, but attentive divers can usually find something of interest. There is no set course for this dive. One way to explore this site: dive along one side of the bay

Route and entry directions
From Victoria one should drive either via Xewkija or Nadur to Qala. Driving via Xewkija one passes through Qala. Coming from Nadur you must turn right in the centre of this village. From here the way to the bay is clearly signposted. The road from Qala meanders down through a series of tight curves to the sea, where you will find a huge car park. Your parking position should be determined by the choice whether to dive from the beach or the quay.

Safety
There are no particular dangers at this site, although currents are possible outside the bay. Boat traffic can be expected.

and then cut across the bay in a zigzag course (maximum depth 10 m) to the other side and from there return to the starting point. There are isolated rock formations with small caves, canyons and also some meadows of sea-grass that help to break the monotony of an otherwise sandy seabed. In the middle of the bay you will find a pipeline. This is the fresh water supply that is pumped across from Malta.

Après diving
During high season there are a number of snack bars to choose from but during the low season it is generally very quiet except at the weekend.

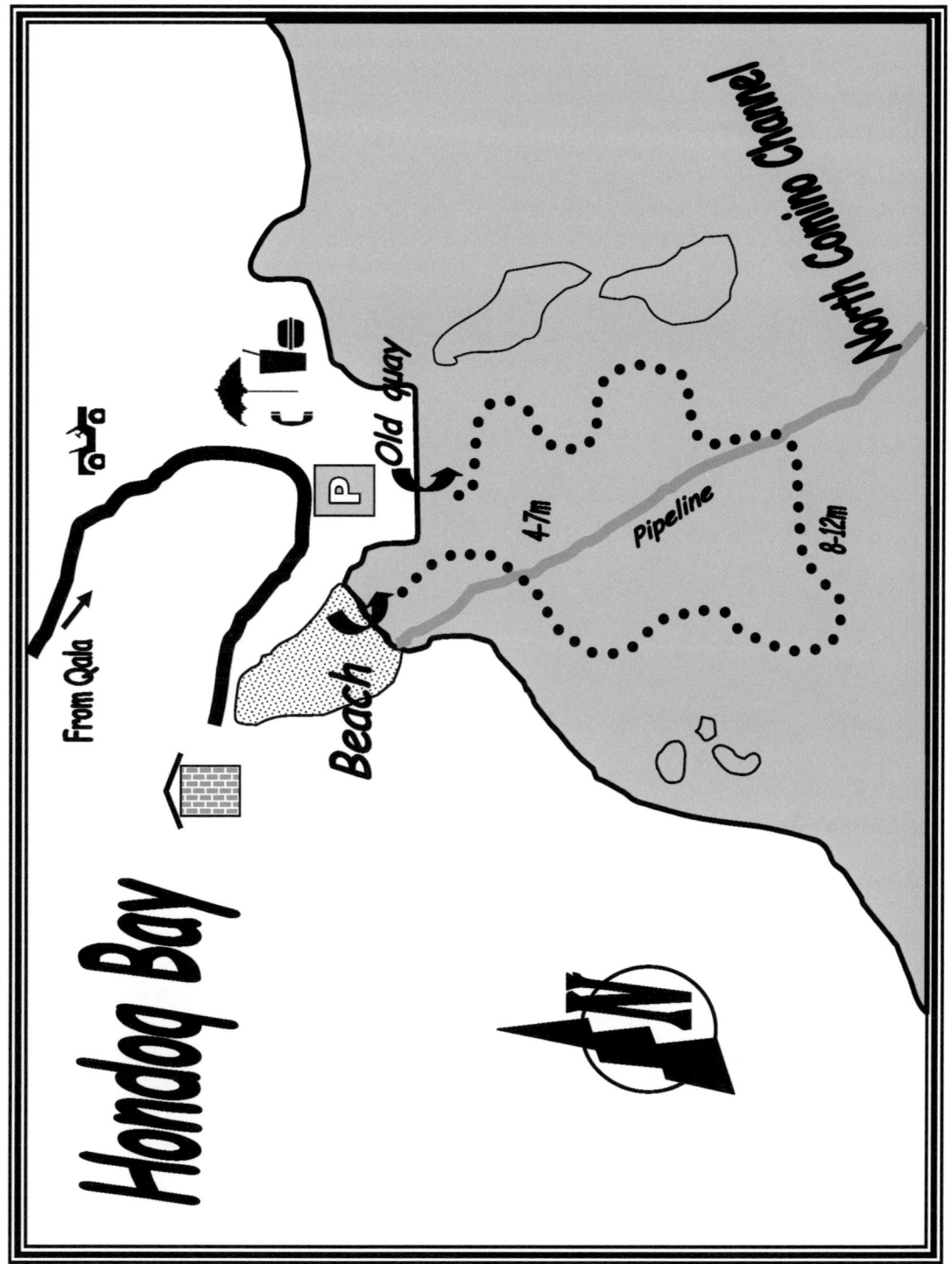

57

Cultural studies

Malta and Gozo

Of course Malta and Gozo offer the traveller far more than just nice diving sites. A trip to the Maltese islands gives one a view of the various different cultures that have presided here through the ages. Apart from diving, one should spend some time to become acquainted with the country and its charming people.

for almost a quarter of the total land area. While Malta is a lively bustling island, Gozo is by contrast a rural area with beautiful undisturbed countryside. Comino is virtually uninhabited.

Life on Gozo is strongly influenced by the constant sunshine in this sub-tropical zone [-> climate]. The prevailing catholic population has nothing in common with the hec-

The Country and its People

The Maltese Archipelago is located at the heart of the Mediterranean, nearly 100 km south of Sicily and 300 km east of Tunisia. Its significant strategic position has been of a great importance since former times.

The combined total area of the two main islands Malta and Gozo is less than a tenth of the size of London. The population density on the island of Malta is similar to any major European city. More than 90 % of the total 375.000 Maltese inhabitants live on this island. The remaining population is sparsely spread over Gozo that accounts

tic way of life found on Malta. The "Gozitans" are distinguished for their charm, kindness and sincerity.

However, living conditions within the Maltese community are far from easy. These limestone islands belong to the European Continental Shelf and tower more than 100 m above the sea. Heat and a lack of water have clearly marked the landscape. Where formerly - about 3000 years ago - forests covered large expanses of land one finds barren rock soil and minimal vegetation and wildlife today.

Summary - Republic of Malta

	Malta (Gozo)
Area:	316 (67) km²
Population:	375.000 (30.000)
Population density:	Approx. 1200 (375) / km²
Religion:	98% catholic
Language:	Maltese and English
Government:	Independent republic since 13.12.1974
Economy:	Tourism, small industrie supplying the EU

The history

Gozo's history is inseparably connected with that of Malta. The islands have been strongly influenced over the centuries since the times of early man. Evidence of prehistoric temples, Arabs, knights and even the British colonial era can still be found on the islands, and their effect on the cultural development is still apparent today. E.g. mementoes of the former British colonies: the English language and the traffic drive on the left. Similarly one finds impressive church domes in almost every village but if one looks more carefully, one also sees architectural elements that were derived from the Arabs.

The islands were inhabited over the centuries as follows:

The first visitors were probably temple architects, who came to the islands about 6000 years ago and merged into the resident population.

During the following centuries they built numerous temples using giant boulders with weights of up to 40 tons. Of the 35 recorded sites a few remnants still exist today. The most impressive historic monument on the Maltese islands is the temple of Ggantija on Gozo. Approximately 1000 B.C. the Phoenicians used the island as a base to extend their sea trade. They were later followed by the Romans who ruled the Maltese islands for approximately 500 years. In the middle of the first century the Apostle Paul was shipwrecked on Malta, which led to founding of the Christian faith on the islands.

The Roman Empire was succeeded by the Byzantine Empire. Later, in the 8th century the Arabs then conquered the islands, but despite almost 200 years of power the Muslims could not suppress the Christian faith of the island's inhabitants. European nobility reigned from the end of the 10th

Historical time schedule of Malta	
Approx. 4000 - 2500 B.C.	Early stone age, (erection of Ggantija), without the use of metal tools
Approx. 2000 - 1000 B.C.	Early bronze age, first evidence of metal craft
Approx. 1000 B.C.	The first Phoenician settlers
218 B.C. - 395 A.D.	The Romans occupy Malta and develop the island to become a trade centre
395 - 869	The Byzantine Empire
870 - 1090	Malta is conquered by Islamic troops and later colonised by the Arabs
1090 - 1530	The Normans and later the Spaniards successively rule the island
1530 - 1798	St. John's Knights rules over the islands
1798 - 1800	Napoleon's troops occupy the island
1800 - 1964	Lord Nelson end the occupation and Malta becomes colony of the UK
1964	Malta earns her independence
1974	Malta becomes Republic
1990	Application for EU membership
2004	Member of European Union 1.1.2008: the Euro becomes official currency

century for the next 450 years, until Charles the fifth eventually gave Malta to the Knights of the Order of St. John.

Many towns and villages (e.g. Valletta and Victoria) still have cultural and religious customs that originate from the realm of the Knights, who settled on Malta in the 16th century. During their 300-year realm they constantly had to defend the island against attacks by the Turks, where they suffered heavy losses, in particular by the great siege of 1565/66.

The reign of the Knights was ended by the invasion of Napoleon's troops in 1798. However they in turn were repelled by British troops who had been summoned to help. As a result, Malta then became a crown colony and a base for the British Navy. During World War II the main island was used as a base by the Allies and was a target for German and Italian air raids for almost two years. At that time, Gozo's remote position was actually an advantage, as it was not considered to be a target and was subsequently ignored during the air raids.

After the war the economy improved. In 1964 Malta became independent. Ten years later the archipelago became a Republic, liberating the islands from the political influence of Great Britain. The next milestone was the full membership in the EU in 2004. As a result of this step the government sources expect a further increase in tourism and an improvement of the economy. On the 1st January 2008 the changeover from the pristine Maltese Pound to the euro took place. The Gozitans are particularly interested to ensure that their island will also profit from the new situation and Gozitan representatives already participate in the Maltese parliament. Gozo's political fate has always been decided on the main island, subject to the mood of the great lords of Malta. Furthermore it was frequently the target of murdering and plundering pirates and armies. Gozo's isolated location and minimal protection, combined with the absence of a safe retreat has led to the population being decimated on a number of occasions.The building of the Citadel finally offered better protection, and even today its walls and bastions still dominate the island's skyline. The fortress, that can be visited today, was constructed in the 17th century and is strategically positioned on a hill in the centre of the island. The offered protection attracted the island's inhabitants to live in the vicinity and led to the establishment of Victoria (Rabat), the present capital. The first recorded settlement on this site dates back to 400 B.C. . Remnants of further settlements, churches and numerous watchtowers dating back to the 16th century can still be found on the island today.

Sights - a trip on Gozo

On Gozo there is perhaps not as much to see as on Malta, but the visitor should at least spend one day sightseeing. At the top of your agenda must be Victoria, the capital of Gozo, with its impressive citadel. Apart from discovering the historical alleys of the old city, one can enjoy a magnificent panoramic view of the whole island from the castle walls. A visit to the cathedral with its false painted "dome" and the natural science museum located nearby is also very informative. Also Victoria's city centre is worth seeing. Apart from the central market place with its numerous cafes and restaurants there are also narrow alleys and squares to ramble through. The shops there offer wines and other local products. Heading east brings you to the city park, which is located behind the bus terminal and the car park. By Mid-European standards the Villa Rundel Garden is not particularly impressive but it holds the region's greatest collection of plants and offers an insight on the local flora. A visit to Ggantija in Xaghra is also an absolute "must", where you will find probably the most impressive Neolithic temple ruins of Malta. This monument was constructed with massive boulders over 5000 years ago. There are also various other impressive ruins on the main island. A lot of questions concerning the builders and their way of life have yet to be answered, but experts are sure that the temples originally had ceilings. Furthermore it is known that priestesses worked there and received messages from the "Great Goddess of Fertility" through slits in the walls. The temples were also used for sacrifices. The old village windmill looks almost modern when compared with this prehistoric monument, however it dates back to the time of the crusades. The windmill has meanwhile been converted into a museum and is well worth a visit. Inside the ancient tower do selections of objects typify rural life during this period. Last but not least Xaghra also has two small stalacmitic caves.

Even more famous is the legendary Calypso Cave, which can be reached in a few minutes from Xaghra. Legend says that Odysseus was kept as prisoner for seven years by the nymph Calypso (as a companion of love). Those who wish to climb down and explore this musty cave ought to take along a flashlight. However, more impressive is the view over the wide sandy beach of Ramla Bay, the largest beach of Gozo. Further east there is nothing of particular interest, but there are some small bays on the north coast (San Blas Bay, Dahlet Qorrot and Qala Point), which are nice for swimming and sun bathing. The next stop should then be in Xewkija with its impressive cathedral that boasts the third largest dome (75m high) in Europe. It was built in 1978 over the structure of the existing church, which was first demolished and then partially rebuilt in a side wing of the cathedral. Surprisingly the building

was financed completely by the 700 inhabitants of the village and not by Rome. Three kilometres down the road is Xlendi, where nature has played her hand to produce a beautiful fjord-like bay. After a country walk along the cliff-tops that in

some places fall 100 m vertically to the sea, one should return to the promenade and enjoy a meal or a drink at one of the numerous restaurants and bars. Further west lays Dwejra Point which offers a concentration of interesting natural landmarks such as the Azure Window, the Inland Sea, the Blue Hole and the Fungus Rock. The latter is called "Il-Gebla tal General", which in Maltese means "Rock of the General". This rock has an extraordinary history. During the Middle Ages a unique medicinal plant "Fungus melitensis" was grown here and the local inhabitants even built a watchtower to ensure that it did not fall into the hands of their enemies.

On your return journey to Victoria you will pass the pilgrimage church of Ta`Pinu, that is situated approximately 500 m to the left of the main road to Victoria. Pilgrims still regularly visit this famous shrine to the Virgin Mary, where a multitude of relics are displayed as evidence of the Virgin's miracles. These are just a few points of interest on Gozo. For detailed information consult one of the guidebooks mentioned in the bibliography.

Travel information from A - Z

- Archaeological discoveries	- Health
- Arrival	- Helicopter service
- Beaches	- Holiday seasons
- Bicycle hire	- Immigration
- Boat hire	- Internet links
- Car hire	- Language
- Clothing/ Diving suites	- Lodging
- Customs and excise	- Maps
- Dining	- Money
- Discos	- Photography
- Drinking water	- Postal/Telephone services
- Electrical supply	- Safety
- Emergency calls	- Sharks
- Environmental protection	- Time shift
- Family vacations	- Traffic regulations
- Ferries Malta - Gozo	- Travel information
- Festivals/ national Holidays	- Travel by bus
- Fuel	- Weather

Archaeological discoveries

Malta has a multitude of archaeological remains; however these are mainly on land. There are few underwater discoveries but it must be pointed out that any findings should be left undisturbed and reported to the local authorities. One known site is in Xlendi Bay, where in order to preserve findings diving inside the south-eastern area in front of the bay is prohibited.

Arrival

Flights to Malta are operated by a number of airlines and charter services. The average flight time to Malta from most European cities is 3 - 4 hours. Upon arrival at Luqa tourists for Gozo generally take a taxi to Cirkewwa and then a ferry to Mgarr. This route is cheap and the trip takes about two hours. Since 2008 there is also a direct bus shuttle form the airport to the ferry harbour. The Gozo-Airport shuttle cost about 5 euro.

Rental cars are available at the airport for those who wish to travel independently. However, one should be aware that traffic on Malta is intense and that the traffic drives on the left [-> Traffic regulations]. My personal recommendation would be to rent a car when you arrive on Gozo and avoid the stress of driving on Malta.

Beaches

Anyone looking for an abundance of large beaches is definitely on the wrong island. Almost the entire Gozo coastline consists of rocky cliffs that are precisely what the diver is looking for. Gozo does however possess one larger sandy beach that can be found at Ramla Bay. There are a handful of smaller bays around the island that are suitable for swimming and sunbathing e.g. Ghasri Valley, Xlendi, Hondoq Bay, Mgarr Ix-Xini and Xlendi Bay. However, none are comparable to the beach of the Blue Lagoon on Comino. Local diving schools and other tourist operations usually arrange trips to the almost uninhabited island. This means that you are rarely alone there! N.B. Nudity and topless bathing is absolutely forbidden!

Bicycle hire
Due to the numerous steep hills, poor road surfaces and the merciless sun Gozo is not suitable for cycling. However, for those who wish to brave these conditions bike hire is available e.g. in Marsalforn, Mgarr, Xlendi and Victoria.

Boat hire
Boat hire on Gozo is possible either with or without a skipper, e.g. at the Inland Sea or in Xlendi. "Xlendi Pleasure Cruises" offers excursions, charter boats and water sports: www.xlendicruises.com. A boat dri-

ving license is needed for boats with more than 4 passengers and power of more than 90 HP.

Car hire
Groups that wish to dive independently will require transportation. A rental car is therefore ideal in order to reach the numerous shore dive sites on the island. Prices are moderate and cars can be reserved in advance through the major car rental offices.

Complete car rental-accommodation-diving packages are meanwhile being offered by hotels and diving schools. Passport and a valid driving license are sufficient for hiring a car, but a minimum age of 21 or occasionally even 25 years is mandatory. In view of the bumpy, sometimes steep and badly maintained roads a jeep is the best choice of vehicle, although more expensive. The big Murati jeeps are suitable for 8 people, respectively for 4 to 5 divers plus luggage. Smaller jeeps for 2 - 3 divers are also available.

Small vans and buses are also frequently offered. They are more spacious than jeeps and have the added security of a closed vehicle but since they have less ground clearance, they are not quite as suitable for the terrain. Full accident insurance is recommended. In the event of an accident the police should always be called to the scene. The RMF breakdown/recovery service is reached on phone: 2155 8844. Occasionally you find an emergency telephone on the roadside.

Clothing/ Diving suits
[-> also weather] High temperatures are possible from the middle of May until October and this should be considered in your choice of clothing. Apart from light long-

sleeved tops, one should not forget to wear a hat. N.B. a light breeze cooling the air can often lead one to neglect sun protection and quickly results in sunburn.

Furthermore it should be remembered that Malta is a catholic country and one should dress appropriately when sightseeing. Women should take care that both shoulders and knees are covered when visiting churches. Nudism and topless bathing is taboo. The necessary respect should be observed, in particular when dressing for a dive.

During spring and autumn it can become considerably cooler through wind and clouds, so be sure to pack a sweater, long trousers and an anorak just in case. A raincoat is seldom required. In wintertime (December to March) heavier clothing is required and a warm windcheater jacket is absolutely essential. Bathing trunks are not required unless you have a heated indoor pool. Concerning diving suits, neoprene should be selected as follows: For autumn, winter and springtime a 7 mm wet or a semi-dry suit is ideal. For the diver that plans either long or frequent dives a dry suit is probably more convenient. In the same sense divers should also consider which gloves to wear. In summer with water temperature up to 27 C, suits can be lighter or possibly even wear a shorty.

During cooler and windy periods and for instance when travelling in an open jeep wear a cap to protect your ears. A jumper or a light anorak is also recommended to avoid cooling after the dive.

Customs and Excise

All personal affects may be imported duty free. Since Malta joined the EU there is free movement of goods between the EU-

countries for personal use. In case of uncertainty please contact your local custom.

Dining

Good wholesome food is available everywhere on the island in all price categories. Gourmets may be difficult to please although there are certainly some tasty dishes. However, the emphasis is on "fast food", i.e. burgers, pizza and fish and chips. Unfortunately very little fresh fish is caught locally so the majority is imported. Where local specialities are offered they may improvise to suit the tourist's taste.

Local specialities such as "Bragioli"(a kind of rolled roasted meat), "Timpaka"(the Maltese variant of the Greek Pastitsjo) or "Lampuka"(a tasty fish dish) are not offered everywhere. To find a suitable restaurant that offers these dishes simply ask a local. Many restaurants are situated directly on the seafront, e.g. in Xlendi or Marsalforn and offer idyllic surroundings, which more than compensate for the sometimes-mediocre food. Enjoy a glass of the local red or white wines in a romantic setting as the day draws to an end.

For those who wish to try something new, try the local non-alcoholic "Kinnie". This bitter-spicy lemonade is a Maltese product made from oranges, water and herbs. The local beer "Cisk Lager" is equally as good as the more expensive import beers.

Discos
Gozo's best-known disco is "La Grotta" which even attracts young people to come over from Malta. This well-known pub, with a cosy open-air terrace, is located on the road from Victoria to Xlendi and is open throughout the high season. Next-door is the equally well-frequented "El Paradiso". N.B. at weekends parking is major problem. Get there early or risk a long walk!

Drinking water
Drinking water is precious on Gozo. The island's water supply is only partially covered by natural resources. More than 60% of demand is extracted from the sea and purified in a desalination plant on Malta and pumped to Gozo via a pipeline (that you can see when diving in Hondoq Bay). This water retains a slight musty flavour but is suitable for consumption. Bottled mineral water is cheap so that may be more convenient when preparing tea or coffee. During heat waves this tends to produce vast amounts of plastic waste!

Visitors are requested to conserve drinking water at all times. This is something to consider when showering or washing down diving equipment. Unfortunately the Maltese people do little to conserve drinking water themselves as one frequently finds dripping taps etc... If you encounter something like this, please do not hesitate to point it out to hopefully make the locals more aware.

Electrical supply
The local electrical supply is 240V AC. Plug sockets are based on British standards so all devices must have a UK three-pin-plugs or an adapter that you can some-

times borrow at the hotel reception. If there is no other way: with some skill it is also possible to plug in the small European standard plug. N.B if electrical devices are not working it may be that there is no current. Many wall sockets are operated with a switch.

Emergency calls
[-> **Emergency procedures last page**]
Emergency services are split into differrent categories.
112 - The national emergency number
191 - Police
199 - Fire
196 or 21556 851 - Ambulance
21561600-Gozo General Hospital w. hyperbaric unit
21244371 - Air rescue
21238797 or 21225040 - Sea rescue
21234766 - Hyperbaric unit (Malta)
Also in case of a diving accident call 112!

To avoid any delays in the rescue chain it is essential that all divers are fully aware of their exact location. As accidents must be reported in English it is recommended (for non-English speakers) to at least learn the most important expressions. In the event of a serious diving accident (decompression sickness, arterial gas embolism) the rescuers must be emphatically informed that it is a diving accident and hyperbaric treatment will be necessary.

Environmental protection
Unfortunately Malta is not renowned for its environmental protection. On the contrary: vehicle exhaust fumes, illegal rubbish dumps and smoking factory chimneys (these are only found on Malta) give clear evidence that, generally speaking, the Maltese people have little regard for their environment. With more than 1200 people

per km² the population density is the highest in the EU. So it isn't easy to solve all problems simultaneously.

Also bird hunting is still very popular even though there are new regulations. Each year hundreds of thousands of birds' are either shot or netted. Not only is this extremely cruel but it could ultimately lead to the extinction of endangered species. Furthermore a vast quantity of poisonous lead finds its way into the soil and water. The situation in the sea appears to be slightly better. This is only because the prevailing currents carry rubbish and sewage away. Over fishing by various nationalities in and around Malta is a further problem.

Malta is also a regular victim of ships illegally discharging bilge tanks and oil. So occasionally small oil slicks may be found, drifting forward the coastline. Unfortunately harpooning is permitted, however only for snorkellers with a license.

On the positive side Gozo has established a protected zone in front of Dwejra Point where fishing with nets is prohibited, so that hopefully larger fish can re-settle there. It is hoped that, after Malta has been admitted to the EU, European environmental standards will be enforced which should result in a number of improvements and also should put an end to bird killing. Individual tourists have little influence on local environmental issues but one should not hesitate to express legitimate concern. After all tourism is Malta's major source of income.

Family vacations
Although the Gozitans are very friendly and love children, Gozo is not really suitable for small children. Day nurseries, babysitter services and recreational facilities for

kids are still extremely rare. Additionally, the excessive heat in summer is probably far too strenuous for toddlers. What activities are offered for children? This rather depends on the age of the children and the time of year. They can swim and play on the beaches (but this is often to hot) or even use the hotel swimming pool.

The cultural highlights are of less interest to children, and also for activities like cycling and skating there are certainly better places than Gozo. However, for youngsters who like water sports there are plenty of opportunities to snorkel or even dive (10 years +).

Ferries Malta - Gozo
Regular services operate during summer (June - September) every 30 to 120 minutes, punctually 24 hours a day. During the winter the frequency is halved and no ser-

Travel information

vices operate between approx. 2 and 5 a.m. . The return fare (around 5 euro per person) is paid on the journey from Gozo to Malta. Cars cost 15 euro (with driver) and kids 1,15 euro. The transfer takes 30 minutes; there is a cafeteria on board. Information is available at the "Gozo Channel Company" in Mgarr Tel: (+356) 21 580435-6, timetable message: 21225016. The current timetable and other information is shown on the Internet under www.gozochannel.com.

Festivals and national holidays

The Gozitans like to celebrate, regardless of whether a religious festival or simply a local fiesta to honour their patron saint takes place. These festivals are not to be missed! The villages are colourfully decorated and everyone has fun in the celebrations that often last the whole weekend. The fiestas always include impressive firework displays.

Official holidays

January 1st: New Years Day
February 10th: St. Paul's shipwreck
March 19th: Feast of St. Joseph
March 31st: Freedom Day to commemorate the withdrawal of the British forces
May 1st: Workers Day
June 7th: Commemoration of the uprising of 1919
June 29th: Feast of St. Peter and St. Paul
August 15th: Feast of the Assumption
September 8th: Feast of our Lady of Victoria, to commemorate the end of the Turkish siege
September 21st: Independence Day
December 8th: The feast of the Immaculate Conception
December 13th: Republic Day
December 25th: Christmas Day

The festival season starts at Munxar on the last weekend of May. This is then followed by Ghasri (1st weekend of June), Xewkija (4th weekend of June), Nadur (29th June), Gharb (1st weekend of July), Kercem (2nd weekend of July), Victoria (3rd weekend of July), Sannat (4th weekend of July), Qala (1st weekend of August), Xlendi (2nd or 3rd weekend of August), Zebbug (20th August), Ghanjsielem (last weekend of August), Xaghra (8th of September).

Fuel

Sometimes petrol stations on Gozo still consist of little more than a single pump on the roadside. There are also some modern stations, e.g. in Victoria and on the road to Mgarr harbour. Outside normal service hours payment is via an unmanned cash/ credit card vendor. Lead free fuel is by now available everywhere, but some of the cars still need leaded fuel(ask at rental station!).

Health
Health conditions on Gozo are the same as in neighbouring Mediterranean countries. No specific vaccinations or inoculations are necessary. The medical systems on both Malta and Gozo are reliable. The greatest health risks are exposure to heat and sunshine. It can be extremely hot in summer, especially in July and August, which can create difficulties for people with circulation problems.

Also divers wearing suits and heavy equipment should be careful to avoid overheating. It is important to avoid exertion and to drink sufficiently (before getting thirsty!).

The intensity of the sun can quickly lead to sunburn. It is therefore essential to use sun-tan lotions with a high protection factor. Additionally one should wear a hat and light long-sleeved clothes.

Helicopter service
This service was discontinued some years ago. For the moment, there is no possibility to reach Gozo via air transportation.

Holiday seasons
During the hottest months July and August a surprisingly large number of guests flock to the islands. Venturing outdoors in the intense heat can be torturous. In the months preceding and following this period the weather is still rather hot but bearable, so this is the recommended time for a diving trip.

From April onwards the weather on Gozo is quite pleasant. The sea is still cool but this has the advantage that most diving sites are then deserted. The sun is already warm enough to sunbathe or to dine outside and the countryside is verdant. This fades as the power of the sun increases each day. The late summer is also quite pleasant. Water temperatures have meanwhile increased (24°C) and this is the best time to find bigger fish.

By the end of September the sun decreases in strength and winds become stronger and more frequent. Occasional showers bring brief relief to the sunburned countryside. Tourists may visit the island the whole year over but by December it

Travel information

becomes cool and most tourist activities close for the winter break. Similarly many dive bases close until the spring. Life on the island slows down during this period so the peace and tranquillity are perhaps an incentive to visit the islands in spite of the rough weather.

Immigration
For residents of the EU a valid identity card or passport is sufficient. N.B. identity cards for children must contain a photo.

Internet links
Malta is geared for tourism and as such presents a variety of information for potential holiday-makers on the web. One finds numerous links with information and advertisements. The selection is vast, e.g.:

General information: www.gozo.com (the homepage for GTA - Gozo Tourism Association), www.visitmalta.com (the homepage for MTA - Malta Tourism Authority), www.exploremalta.com (a search engine, for commercial links), www.dive-gozo.com (the author's homepage with detailed information and photos

Weather: www.gozo.ws
Outdoor sports: www.gozoadventure.com
Official: www.gozo.gov.mt
Environment and nature: www.naturetrust-malta.org, www.eco-gozo.gov.mt
News: www.gozonews.com

Language
Although Maltese is the official language almost all Gozitans speak English, the second national language. Even anyone that speaks only a little English need not to despair, as the friendly Gozitans will be happy to assist you. For those wishing to understand the language, beware! Modern day Maltese is originally derived from the Phoenician language. Over the centuries Latin, Arabic, Italian and even English have influenced this difficult dialect. An example: try pronouncing "Tejjipx" - which means "no smoking".....

Fortunately only a little skill is required to pronounce the village names correctly.

Qala	A-la
Ggantija	jan-tee-ya
Xaghra	Sha-ra
Zebugg	Za-boosh
Ghammar	Am-mar
Gharb	Arb
Xlendi	Shlen-dy
Munxar	Moon-shar
Mgarr	Em-jarr
Xewkija	Shev-kee-ya

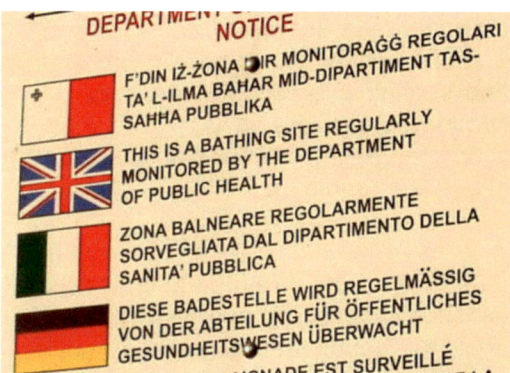

Lodging
Accommodation on Gozo is constantly increasing but there are no plans to open Gozo for cheap package holidays. The Gozitans think more in terms of quality rather than quantity. Divers may find accommodation ranging from inexpensive apartments and boarding houses to the more exclusive hotels or idyllically situated cottages. The most popular holiday locations on Gozo are in Marsalforn and Xlendi, where the infrastructure is already quite sophisticated.

One can quickly find suitable accommodation using tourist offices or via the Internet. Many diving schools also offer complete packages including accommodation. During the hot summer months accommodation that includes the use of a swimming pool is recommended. Families and groups will find that hiring apartments and small cottages probably offers the best value for money.

Maps
There is a new detailed roadmap issued by RMF (a car break-down agency based on Malta). You can obtain another good map of Gozo (Scale 1:25000, publisher: Miller Guides) quite cheaply from most local stores. This is indispensable for a detailed exploration of the island [-> Bibliography].

Money
Since 1st of January 2008 the official currency on Malta is the Euro. Because tourism plays a major role in the Maltese economy, exchange is no problem, either directly at the airport (cash, traveller cheques, EC or credit card) or directly on Gozo, where one can find numerous banks and cash machines in Victoria, Marsalforn and Xlendi. Also many hotels, restaurants shops and diving centres accept the major credit cards.

Photography
No holiday is complete without photographs. Since digital photography is very popular, traditional films are hard to get. It is best to bring your own films with you and have them developed at home, but if necessary standard film material is also available on Gozo. Facilities to develop slide films or to purchase more specific materials are available on Malta. For tourists with digital cameras there are several shops for instant printing e.g. in Victoria.

Postal & telephone services
Postage stamps are available at post offices, hotels and anywhere you can buy postcards. Telephone cards may be purchased at chemists, kiosks or at the hotel reception.

The international dialling code in Malta is 00 (like the rest of Europe) + country code + area code (without zero) + number. Cheap rates are available between 9 p.m. and 6 a.m. . Calling Malta from abroad, dial +356.

Travel information

Malta has meanwhile an extensive mobile telephone network but one should check if your provider is supported locally. If you plan to use mobile phones for emergencies check the reception beforehand. The local companies like Go Mobile, Vodafone etc. offers also prepaid cards, internet connections and other multimedia services (if you need this at your holidays).

Safety
Until recently Gozo had virtually no criminality. Unfortunately petty thievery has found its way to the island. Where previously one could simply leave their belongings in an open jeep and go diving it is no longer recommendable these days. Leave valuables at the hotel unless you have a vehicle that can be locked and valuables are hidden from view.

Sharks
Yes! There are sharks! Approximately 50 species of sharks are known in the Mediterranean. However divers rarely glimpse these fascinating creatures. The deep trench between Malta and Sicily offers ideal living conditions for a number of different breeds including "jaws", the great white. In 1977 a specimen of 7 m was caught by a local fisherman.

Due to over-fishing the tuna shoals have been decimated and the basic food item for the sharks has been reduced. Although an encounter with a shark remains possible, it is extremely unlikely as sharks seldom venture into shallow water. With a little luck one may observe blue shark, dogfish as well as tope and mako.

Time shift
On Gozo the time is GMT + 1 hour. In summer an additional hour has to be added.

However, an ancient somewhat confusing tradition can be witnessed on Gozo and Malta, where clocks on twin-towered churches indicate different times with the idea the devil should be confuse and prevented from disturbing Mass.

Traffic regulations
Despite the impression one gets there are traffic regulations! Traffic drives on the left (no problem for visitors from the UK). For those not used to right-hand drive vehicles it is advisable to get acquainted with the controls before venturing onto the road.

Traffic from the right has right of way! Roundabouts should be circumnavigated in a clockwise direction. Any traffic on a roundabout automatically has right of way over vehicles wishing to enter. N.B. Beware - busses seem to have their own "built-in right of way"!

The speed limit is 50 km/h in cities and 80 km/h outside. The blood alcohol limit is 80 millilitres.

Travel by bus
For those with time to spare and who would like to explore the island without a car, the colourful ancient Gozo buses are an interesting alternative. Pay the driver upon boarding and for just 50 cents you

are relieved of the problem of facing the local traffic.

Timetables are available at the Victoria and Mgarr bus station or - sometime - in the bus. If there is no plan the friendly Gozitians will be happy to help you. Bus stops are marked with blue signs and all bus lines lead to the central bus terminal in Victoria. This is perhaps not the most com-fortable mode of transport but interesting all the same.

Travel information
The MTA (Maltese Tourism Authority) offers a variety of detailed information for travel within the islands. On Gozo: Victo-ria, Tigrija Palazz, Level 1, Republic Street, (+356) 21 561419. Free hotline: 8007 2230. Other offices are at the airport and in Valetta. Email: info@visitmalta.com, www.visitmalta.com

The MTA also has a representation in most European countries. They are usually very helpful with general queries but cannot answer specific diving issues. Therefore, ask the local diving facilities.

Weather
[-> also holiday seasons]
The Maltese climate is characterised by very hot and dry summers and fresh, windy and humid winters. Springtime and autumn are the most agreeable periods with a lot of warm days and little rain. It is windy most of the year and hefty storms can occur quite suddenly.

The following chart indicates the most important average weather conditions:

1) Average max. temperatures (C)
2) Average min. temperatures (C)
3) Daily sunshine (hours)
4) Average number of rainy days
5) Average water temperatures (C)

		Jan	Feb	Mar	Apr	May	Jun	Jul	Aug	Sep	Oct	Nov	Dec
Day	1)	14	14	16	18	22	26	29	29	27	24	19	16
Night	2)	10	10	11	13	16	19	22	23	22	19	15	12
Sun	3)	6	6	8	9	10	12	13	12	9	8	6	5
Rain	4)	12	7	6	4	2	0	0	1	3	9	10	12
Water	5)	15	14	15	15	18	21	24	25	24	22	19	17

Bibliography

Bibliography

<u>Marine biology</u>

Campbell, A.C.
Mediterranean Sea
Hamlyn Publishing Group Ltd., London 1982
ISBN 0-600-36417-8
-> A guide to the marine biology

Lanfranco, Guido G.
The Fish around Malta
Progress Press Ltd, Malta, 1996

Moosleitner, Horst/ Patzner Robert
Underwater Guide Mediterranean - Fish
(German /English)
Delius Klasing Verlag/ Edition Naglschmid,
Germany 2001, ISBN 3-89534-001-1

Moosleitner, Horst/ Patzner Robert
Underwater Guide Mediterranean - Invertebrates (German /English)
Delius Klasing Verlag/ Edition Naglschmid,
Germany 1995, ISBN 3-89594-000-3

Mojetta, Angelo
Mediterranean Sea Guide to the Underwater Life
Swan Hill Press, 1996

Debelius, Helmut
Mediterranean and Atlantic fish guide
IKAN UW-Archiv (Germany)

<u>Other diveguides:</u>

Wood, Lawson & Lesley
The dive sites of Malta, Gozo and Comino
New Holland Publishers (UK) Ltd, 1999
ISBN 99909-3-054-6 New edition 2006

Middleton, Ned
Maltese Islands Diving Guide
White Star S.r.L (Italy), 1997

Lemon, Peter G.
Shore Diving the Maltese Islands
Lavenham Press Limited (GB), 2007

<u>Malta/ Gozo guidebooks:</u>

National Tourism Organisation
Malta, a guide to the islands

Richards, Brian
Globetrotter Travel Guide to Malta
New Holland Publishers, London

Borg, Victor Paul
The rough guide to Malta & Gozo
Rought guides Ltd. PB, 2001

Cini, Charles
Gozo - a journey to the past
1992

Ross, Geoffrey A.
Malta, Gozo & Comino: a travel portrait
Nomad, 2001
(available in 5 Languages: English, French, German, Italian, Dutch)

Maps:
Gozo, Comino Comprehensive Map 1:25.000, Miller Guides, Malta

Gozo Map 1:25.000, RMF, Malta 2001

Globetrotter Travel Map Malta
New Holland Publishers, London

Light fiction :
Bradford, Ernle
The Great Siege - Malta 1565
ISBN: 014002106

Pickles, Tim
Malta 1565

Hammett, Dashiell
The Maltese Falcon

Hamilton. Lyn
The Maltese Goddess: An Archaeological Mystery Mass Market Paperback, 1998

Outdoor sport:

Hancock, Xavier
Gozo Adventures Guidebook
Diving, rock climbing, hiking, biking
Malta

Multimedia:
Sedlitzki, Stephan., Tegge, Klaus-Thorsten
DVD: **Diving around Gozo**: Video impressions, pictures & divesites expositions,
www.dive-gozo.com

Hutter, Frederic
CD-Rom: panoround GOZO & COMINO
Virtuel travel guide with 360° pictures

Diving facilities & accomodation tips:

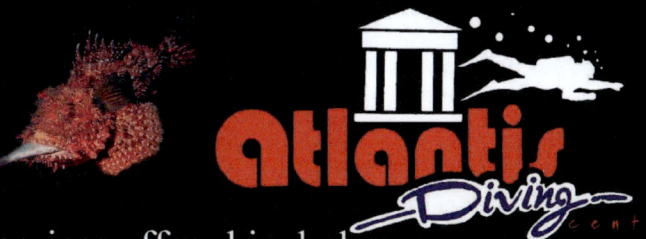

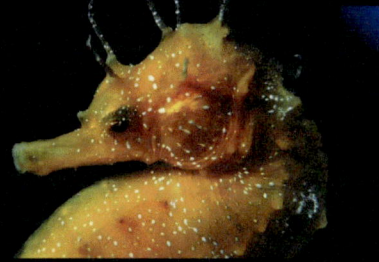

Recommendations

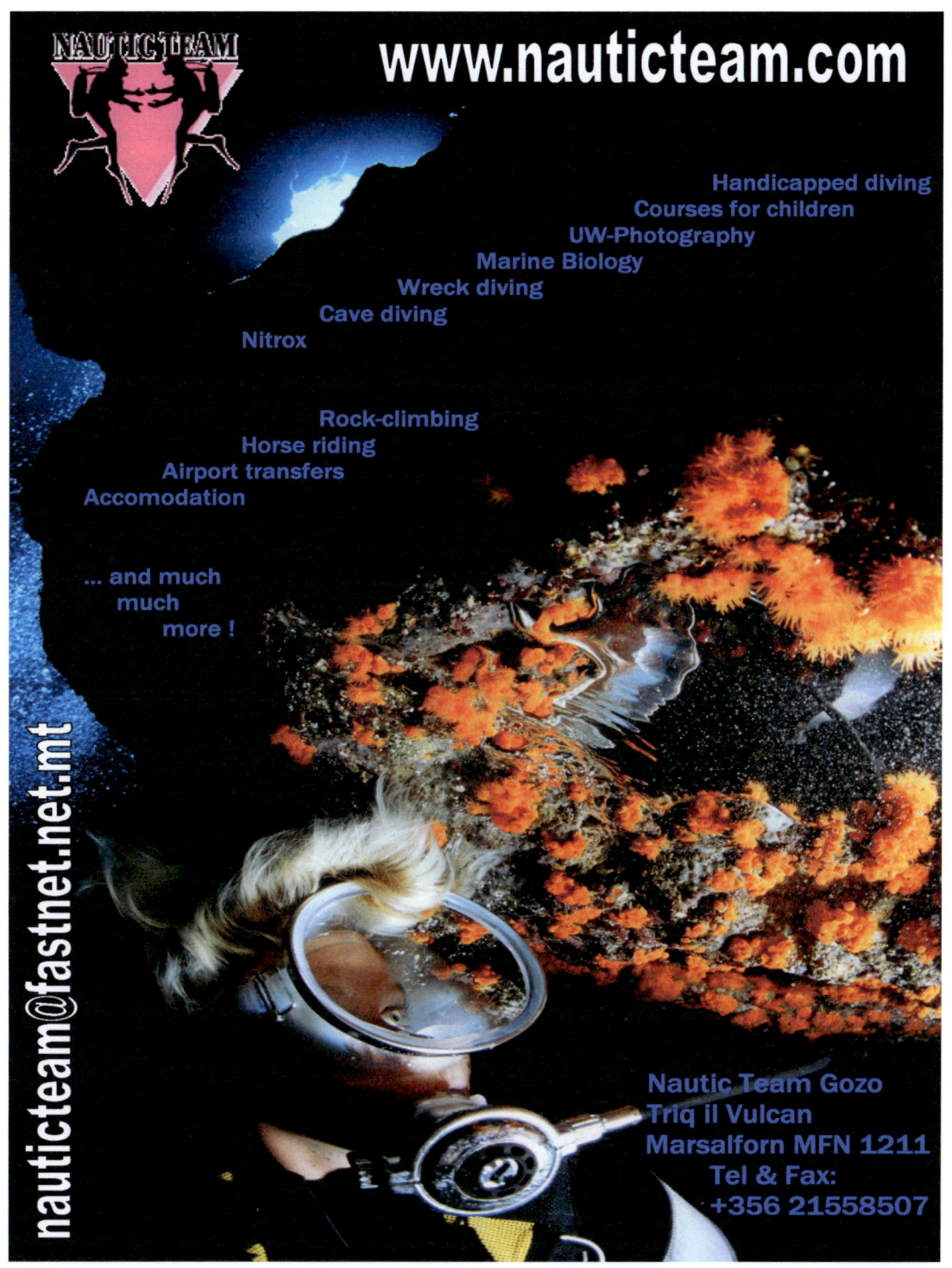

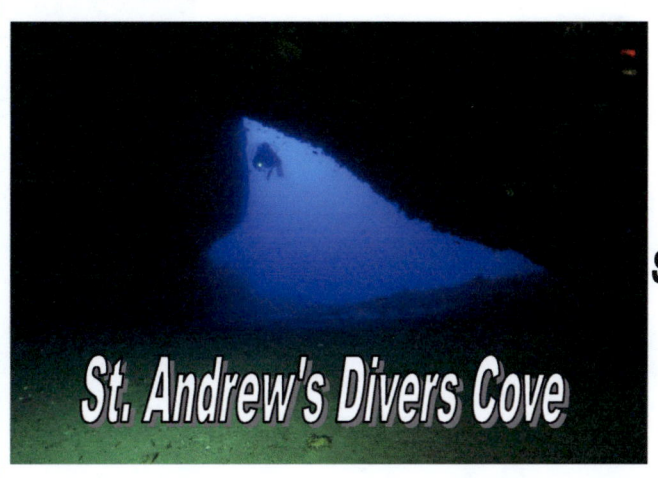

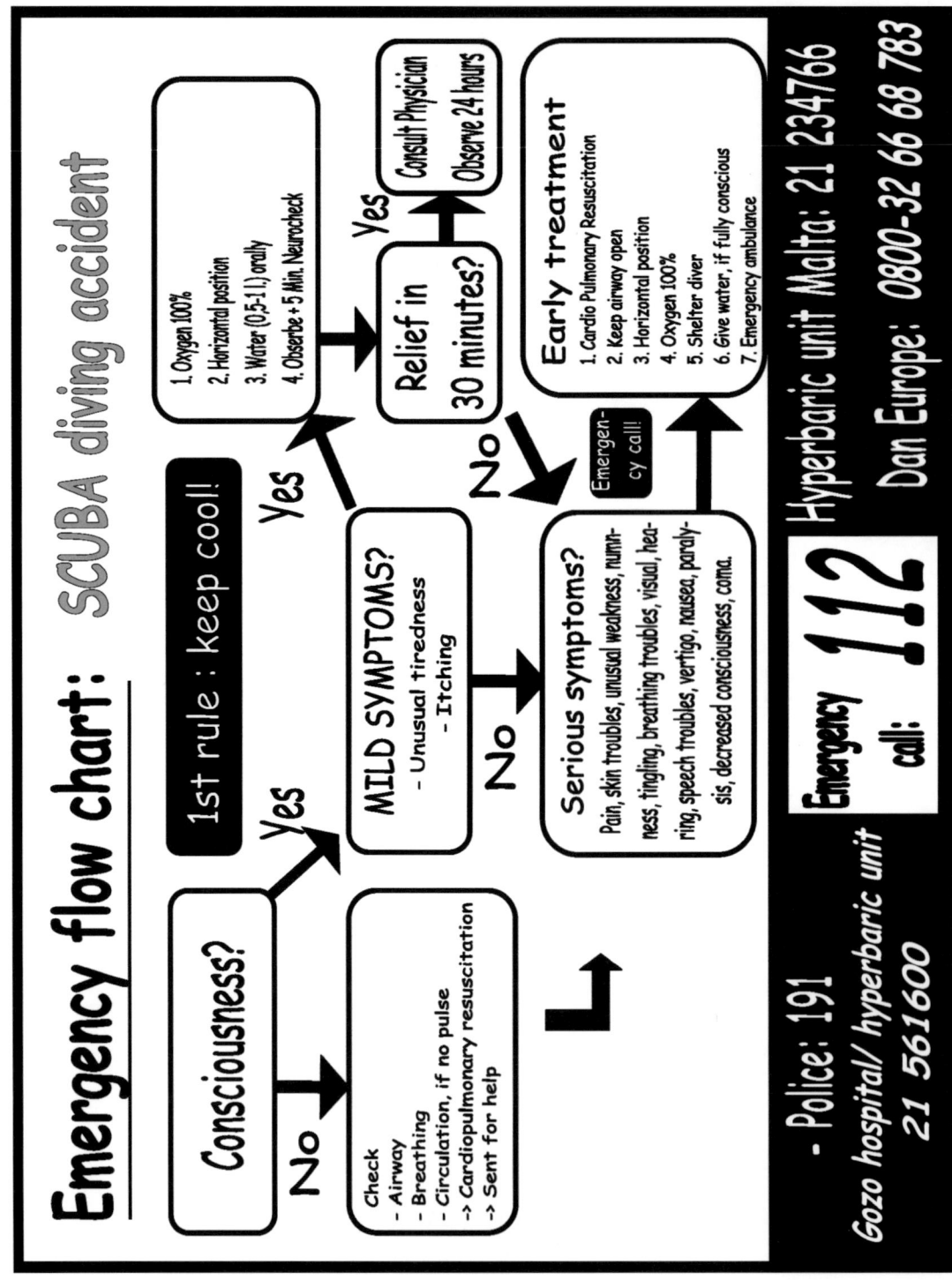

Emergency flow chart: SCUBA diving accident

1st rule : keep cool!

Consciousness?

No →

Check
- Airway
- Breathing
- Circulation, if no pulse
→ Cardiopulmonary resuscitation
→ Sent for help

Yes →

MILD SYMPTOMS?
- Unusual tiredness
- Itching

Yes →

1. Oxygen 100%
2. Horizontal position
3. Water (0,5-1 l.) orally
4. Observe + 5 Min. Neurocheck

Relief in 30 minutes?

Yes → Consult Physician / Observe 24 hours

No →

No →

Serious symptoms?
Pain, skin troubles, unusual weakness, numbness, tingling, breathing troubles, visual, hearing, speech troubles, vertigo, nausea, paralysis, decreased consciousness, coma.

Emergency call!

Early treatment
1. Cardio Pulmonary Resuscitation
2. Keep airway open
3. Horizontal position
4. Oxygen 100%
5. Shelter diver
6. Give water, if fully conscious
7. Emergency ambulance

Emergency call: 112

- Police: 191

Gozo hospital/ hyperbaric unit 21 561600

Hyperbaric unit Malta: 21 234766

Dan Europe: 0800-32 66 68 783